*The Exercise of
Influence
in Small Groups*

Terence K. Hopkins
Columbia University

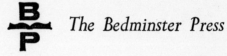 The Bedminster Press

The Exercise of
Influence
in Small Groups

To the memory of E.M.H.

Acknowledgments

The essay which follows began in 1956, when I was working with Robert K. Merton in his seminar on organization theory and with Herbert H. Hyman in his seminar on evaluation research. My very considerable debts to them cannot be discharged through a note such as this, but at least some I am conscious of can be recorded. In substance, as will soon become evident, the essay draws much and often on Merton's ideas; and such coherence as it exhibits results largely from exploring some of the reaches of his well-known paradigm for the sociological analysis of functional systems. To Hyman I owe especially my handling of evidence, in particular the summaries of findings here which are modeled directly after the summaries in his *Political Socialization* (1959). The essay would not be what it is without these intellectual guides. But it would not have come into being at all without the warm skepticism, the balanced combination of personal friendship and impersonal criticism, which each in his own way has shown and in the process taught me to respect.

In 1957-58, I held a pre-doctoral research training fellowship from the Social Science Research Council, and I wish to express my thanks to the Council for this year.

It was largely spent in close collaboration with Morris Zelditch, Jr. (then at Columbia, now at Stanford), who contributed so materially to my thinking in this period that I find it difficult to distinguish between his influence and whatever "normal growth" I experienced at the time. I am aware, however, that his work is a principal source of my discussion of the properties of small groups and in particular of my comments on interaction and its measurement; and his critical reading of earlier drafts forced me to eliminate many irrelevancies from the text and to clarify as many ambiguities.

In 1959 I submitted a version of this work as my Ph.D. dissertation at Columbia. I am grateful to the members of the examining committee—Conrad M. Arensberg, Paul F. Lazarsfeld, Robert K. Merton, David B. Truman, Morris Zelditch, Jr.

and Hans L. Zetterberg—for the careful reading each gave the manuscript and the many detailed comments each made.

Hans L. Zetterberg's part has been as many-sided as possible. To begin with, he provided through his book *On Theory and Verification in Sociology* the main stimulus for the way I have handled the principal concepts and propositions. He sponsored the essay and guided its completion as a dissertation. He subsequently continued to be its sponsor in effect, for in the period since then he has been a constant source of counsel, encouragement, and support. And finally, he has been its principal editor, having read, criticized, and commented on all the various revisions, additions, and proposed deletions as they have been made. As teacher, colleague, and friend he has contributed so substantially to the content of this work that no acknowledgment can possibly convey how much it owes to his efforts.

It would be remiss of me not to mention briefly four others to whom I am also indebted, although their considerable influence is but indirectly reflected in the present work.

Harvey Goldberg (then at Oberlin, now at Wisconsin) and Sherwood Fox (then at New York, now at Union) interrupted a cheerfully wayward existence and in due course secured a convert.

William J. Goode introduced me to sociological analysis, taught me by precept, example, and patience the use of theory in the conduct of research, and has over the years given freely of both his ideas and his counsel.

The late Karl Polanyi, now retired from Columbia, taught me the meaning of scholarship. In the nature of the case, few students can spend their graduate years in the company of a great scholar, and I am deeply grateful for having had that rare privilege.

Contents

The Exercise of
Influence
in Small Groups

[1]

Introduction

We must not say that an action shocks the common conscience because it is criminal but rather that it is criminal because it shocks the common conscience. . . .

If, then, when it is committed, the consciences which it offends do not unite themselves to give mutual evidence of their communion . . . they would be permanently unsettled. They must reinforce themselves by mutual assurances that they are always agreed. . . .

We can thus say without paradox that punishment is above all designed to act upon upright people, for, since it serves to heal the wounds made upon collective sentiments, it can fill this role only where these sentiments exist, and commensurately with their vivacity.

Emile Durkheim, *The Division of Labor in Society*

In virtually all groups some members exercise more influence than others. Differences among members in this respect may be considerable or slight, permanent or transient, but they are present in most groups most of the time. This book attempts to answer two questions about such differences: What factors govern the distribution of influence among the members of a group? Under what conditions does this distribution remain relatively stable?

The analysis proceeds in two steps, corresponding to these two questions. The first and longer part presents a set of propositions describing the relationships among four properties of the status of member—rank, centrality, conformity, and observability—and between each of these and the influence a member exercises. The propositions are considered in some detail, each being weighed against current theory for its reasonableness and against available data for its plausibility.

In the second part the propositions are related to a basic group process, the principal tendency of which is to bring into balance, over a group's set of members, the distributions of rank and of influence. When members' ranks and degrees of influence are highly correlated, one may speak of a "legitimate" structure of influence, the state of legitimacy being one condition of stability. The tendency toward legitimacy, however, is seldom realized because the operation of the process more often than not interferes with other processes serving other functional requirements of group stability. The analysis in this part therefore focuses on various institutional and structural features of groups that, as mechanisms constraining the process or mitigating its effects, help stabilize the distribution of influence short of full legitimacy.

The focus on stability, I should point out, is entirely heuristic. No assumption is made that groups always or usually exhibit stable influence structures. On the contrary, as the analysis suggests, instability rather than stability is probably the more common state, most groups being able to provide the conditions for stable influence structures for brief periods only.

The Exercise of Influence in Groups

The concept of influence informing the essay differs from most current conceptions. The latter are concerned with the attitudinal and behavioral effects of one person upon another. Groups, not persons, form the subject matter of this essay, however, and a concept of influence useful for studying its exercise in groups, as opposed to interpersonal relations, is needed. The sort of concept I think necessary occurs in Durkheim's thesis regarding crime and punishment, which is outlined in the excerpts heading the chapter, and the concept used here derives from his formulations, especially those in the analysis of punishment. As a response to crime, he reasons, punishment undoubtedly plays:

. . . a useful role. Only this role is not where we ordinarily look for it. It does not serve or only serves quite secondarily to correct the guilty person or to intimidate his possible imitators; from either point of view, its efficacy is justly doubtful and, in any case, mediocre. Its true function is to maintain social cohesion intact by preserving all the vitality of the common conscience. Denied so categorically, the latter would necessarily lose its vigor if an emotional reaction of the community did not arise to make up for the loss, and a slackening of social solidarity would result. It is necessary therefore that it be spiritedly affirmed the instant it is contradicted, and the only way for it to be affirmed is the expression of the unanimous aversion, which the crime continues to inspire, by a positive act which can only consist in inflicting pain on the agent. Thus, although a necessary product of the causes which occasion it, this pain is not a gratuitous cruelty. It is the sign which certifies that the collective sentiments are still collective . . . and in this way it repairs the harm which the crime has done society. . . . Without this necessary satisfaction, what we call the moral conscience could not be maintained (Emile Durkheim, *De la Division du travail social*, Book 1, Chapter 1, Section 4)[1].

The essential point seems clear. In the analysis of society, the functionally significant effects of crime and punishment are the effects they have upon collective sentiments, not those they have upon particular individuals.

It is this general orientation that I propose to use in defining influence. The relevant criterion of its exercise in a group thus becomes the effect an action has on the members viewed collectively, in particular the effect it has on the content and relative salience of shared norms. In turn, a member exercises more or less influence depending on the impact his actions have upon consensus, upon commonly held sentiments and opinions, whatever effects they may have on specific other members.

There is of course an intimate relationship between the norms of a group and the attitudes of its members taken severally. As-

---

[1] The standard translation gives, I think, an inadequate and confusing rendering of this important passage. Compare Durkheim, 1947, pp. 108-109.

sumptions to this effect underlie most methods of measuring group opinion or sentiment, and their counterpart in theory, called by Parsons the "theorem of institutional integration" (1951, pp. 36-45), occupies a prominent place among the fundamental ideas of modern sociology. Group norms and individual attitudes are not identical: Each member of just about any group probably both holds some attitudes that are not normative in the group and fails to hold some attitudes that are normative. The two are closely related, however, and there cannot be effects on group norms that are not accompanied by some sort of parallel effects on the attitudes of one or more of the participating individuals.

For this reason, to say that influence refers to the observed or imputed effects of actions on a group's state of consensus entails no major methodological difficulties. No new logic of inference is required in order to move from concept to observation or from observation to concept. The procedures ordinarily used to infer that an individual's attitudes have been influenced are the same, in principle, as those used to infer that a group's norms have been influenced. Nor are new kinds of observations necessarily called for. Many of those now used to indicate the exercise of influence in interpersonal relations can serve also to indicate its exercise in groups. All that the conception entails is that an interpretation somewhat different from the usual one be placed on the observations that are made, and consequently that the observations be arranged for analysis in a somewhat different form and that the analysis itself pursue a somewhat different course.

It might be noted that influence in this view attaches conceptually to acts of members rather than to members directly. Strictly speaking, acts are influential, not members. This is a useful formulation for some purposes, but for most it is cumbersome, and so, in line with Parsons' suggestion that often "it is convenient to make use of a higher order unit than the act, namely, the status-role" (Parsons, 1951, p. 25), the exercise of influence is usually treated as a property of the status (or role) of group member.

Theoretical Approach

The theory developed here differs in approach not only from the "trait" theories, common until recently in psychology and sociology, and from the "situational" theories, current in modern social psychology. It also differs in approach from most contemporary sociological theories of influence insofar as they are patterned after Weber's views on authority and legitimation and propose to account for a group's distribution of influence primarily in terms of its common values and normative role-expectations.

For the purpose of this analysis, I conceive of the interaction system of a group rather narrowly, as including only group properties of a specifically structural or formal nature (e.g., frequency of interaction among members). Variables referring to personality characteristics of members (e.g., authoritarianism) or to cultural features of groups (e.g., egalitarian norms) are treated as external to the interaction system. Many factors which in other studies are viewed as within the system, or as directly affecting the distribution of influence among the members of a group, are thus viewed here for analytic purposes as in the system's environment and as having only indirect effects on influence—through the conditioning effects they have on the set of relationships among the structural variables.

Distinguishing between the specifically cultural or psychological and the specifically structural or formal is thus basic both to the theory and to the method of analysis developed here, and a brief discussion of the matter in more general terms may prove helpful. As was said, the theory formulates an answer to the question, What determines the distribution of influence among the members of a group? In sociology there have traditionally been two rather different modes of answering questions of this sort.

In one, the analyst describes various values, sentiments, beliefs, and uses them to explain observed patterns of behavior—in the present case, the way influence is distributed over the membership of a group or the observed stability of the distribution. For example, he might cite the relevant differences in these respects between groups with bonapartist ideologies and groups with anarchist ideologies. In essentials, this is the method Weber follows in constructing the three types of authority. He first describes three different kinds of value systems, the rational or legal, the traditional, and the charismatic, and then discusses the differences in structure—in the relations between the supreme head and the administrative staff and between the staff and the members of the subject population—that presumably correlate with the differences in values (Weber, 1947, pp. 324-363). Toennies also proceeds in this way most of the time, as does Parsons.

If instead of cultural elements one uses psychological elements, such as basic needs, personality traits, and so on, where these have definite content, the procedure in outline is much the same. Redl's characterization of types of "central persons" and correlative "group formations" is of this kind (Redl, 1942).

The alternative to this way of answering the question is to work with concepts that are devoid of *particular* cultural or psychological content. For example, the analyst of the formal persuasion might say that the distribution of influence remains relatively stable, whatever the ideology of the group or the character structure of the participants, so long as those who exercise the most influence occupy the highest-ranking positions and those who exercise the least influence, the lowest-ranking positions. The particular values in terms of which rank is accorded, or the particular need-dispositions leading some members to look up to others, are irrelevant.

A good statement on the purpose of this kind of analysis occurs in the editors' Introduction to *African Political Systems*.

After noting that the papers in the volume omit materials ordinarily found in anthropological accounts, Fortes and Evans-Pritchard point out that the comparative study of political systems:

> . . . has to be on an abstract plane where social processes are stripped of their cultural idiom and are reduced to functional terms. The structural similarities which disparity of culture conceals are then laid bare and structural dissimilarities are revealed behind a screen of cultural uniformity (Fortes and Evans-Pritchard, 1940, p. 3).

In essentials, this mode of analysis is used extensively by Simmel (1950), Barnard (1938), Nadel (1957), and to some extent by Homans (1950). It is also the mode of analysis used here.

A Sketch of the Theory

The structural features of groups that are singled out for attention are four: a group's rank structure or, loosely, its "stratification"; its structure or network of interaction; the visibility it affords members of events and conditions in the group; and its sphere of normative consensus. These of course imply substantive content of a psychological or cultural nature and could be described and analyzed in terms of such content. But they are treated formally here, the group properties which interest us being the stability of the rankings, the frequency with which members interact, the level of visibility in the group, and the degree of normative consensus among the members. Like influence, each of these is translated into a property of the status of member and viewed as a dimension along which the members of a group may vary relative to one another. The determinants of a member's degree of influence thus become his relative rank or standing in the group, his frequency of participating (or "centrality," as it is designated here), his degree of observability, and his degree of normative conformity.

These are all held to be causally relevant to a member's degree of influence, but for reasons given later, they are also held to be related to one another and to influence in a certain order or sequence. Briefly, rank is seen to lead to centrality, centrality to observability and conformity, these to influence, then influence back to rank, and so on. It is this set of sequential relations that presumably describes a basic process of groups the main tendency of which is to bring into balance over a group's membership the distributions of rank and of influence.

This set of relations among structural variables is also the one through which psychological, cultural, and situational factors have effects on the distribution of influence in a group. The variables of the process—rank, centrality, observability, conformity, and influence—are related not only to one another but also to numerous factors outside the system. Variations in these external factors thus tend to bring about variations in the factors within the system and hence to affect the way the process operates. By introducing into the analysis various psychological, cultural, and situational factors that are said to have important effects on the distribution of influence, one can examine whether and to what extent they do have these effects and can describe the causal sequences through which they probably produce them.

One kind of indirect effect from external factors is of particular theoretical interest. The concept of legitimacy, as usually defined, implies a high correlation between the status-properties of rank and influence. The strength of the correlation between them may therefore be used as an indicator of the degree of legitimacy of an influence structure. In turn, then, the rank-influence process may be viewed as continually tending to produce the condition of legitimacy, irrespective of the content of the particular normative or value patterns that happen to be institutionalized in a group. Except under special circumstances, though, this process does not tend to maintain the rank and influence of any one member at a particular level. It only tends to maintain a positive relationship between the two properties. The very tendency to bring them into balance, that is, the very tendency toward legitimacy, can thus prove to be a basic source of instability in groups. This is so partly because any substantial re-ranking of members is likely to prove highly disruptive, and partly because the process may prove disruptive in other ways, for example, by generating a difference between higher- and lower-ranking members that is too great relative to some required degree of group solidarity, or too little relative to some required degree of orderliness in interaction. The indirect effects that are of special interest are those that tend to counteract the process or to constrain it. Several institutional features commonly found in groups seem to have such effects, as the analysis shows. These features, under certain conditions, help to maintain a given degree of legitimacy by nullifying the effects of potentially disturbing variations or, under other conditions, help to anchor the exercise of influence in particular statuses even though a group's distribution of influence lacks full legitimacy.

Outline of the Book

In Chapter 2, several basic concepts are introduced, including *group, small group* (since the theory is applied here only to the exercise of influence in small groups), and *group member,* as well as *rank, centrality, conformity,* and *observability.* In Chapter 3, the propositions linking the five status-properties are stated and then examined in the light of current theory and such systematic evidence as is available. The set of assertions is used in Chapter 4 first to derive a structural concept of leadership and then to account for the effectiveness of an opinion change program. In Chapter 5, it is construed as depicting the process through which rank and influence tend to be equilibrated; some of the dysfunctions of the resultant tendency to maintain or develop the state of legitimacy are described; and various features of groups that may function to curtail the operation of the process or to soften its negative effects are discussed. Chapter 6 concludes the essay with a brief summary.

[2]

Some Basic Concepts

In a given context of inquiry, and in the light of the problems which initiate it, there may be ample justification for ignoring all but one system of activities to whose maintenance things and processes contribute. But such disregard of other wholes and of other functions which their constituents may have, does not warrant the conclusion that what is ignored is less genuine or natural than what receives selective attention.

Ernest Nagel, *"Teleological Explanation and Teleological Systems"*

The first part of this chapter discusses the concepts of group, small group, and group member, the second takes up the concepts of rank, centrality, observability, and conformity, and the third develops further the concept of influence.

Concepts of Units

Group

Following Merton, we can say that a number of people constitute a group if they (1) "interact with one another in accord with established patterns," (2) "define themselves as 'members,' i.e., . . . have patterned expectations of forms of interaction which are morally binding on them and on other 'members' but not on those regarded as 'outside' the group," and (3) are "defined by others as 'belonging to the group' " (Merton, 1957, pp. 285-286).

As this formulation clearly implies, the criteria used to decide whether a particular set of people constitutes a sociological group entail matters of degree. In this case, to make a rough translation, they are the degree of consensus among the participants on the "morally binding" or normative expectations, the degree to which interaction in fact occurs, the degree to which it occurs in accord with the expectations commonly considered binding, and the degree to which participants define themselves and are defined by others as constituting a collective entity or social unit.[1]

"Normative consensus" usually refers to the set of ideas and sentiments that members feel each should hold, express, or live up to in virtue of his membership and that most of them in fact do hold. In general, it is assumed that this consensus is subject to a sort of law of social entropy, that a group's normative consensus tends not to remain intact but to disintegrate and that it does disintegrate in the absence of identifiable mechanisms of

[1] These criteria, especially the first two, are not unidimensional concepts but broad, multi-dimensional concepts, despite the use of the term "degree." "Normative consensus" contains at least four distinct dimensions. There is the *normative* component, referring to ideas and sentiments that the participants in a group (a) are expected as members to hold, express, and act in accordance with, and (b) have internalized or "integrated" with the need-dispositions of their personality systems (Parsons, 1951). An idea or sentiment is thus more or less normative in a group depending upon whether holding it is, one, an obligation of membership and, two, a psychological condition of each participant which exists in principle independently of his membership in the group in question (although it may initially be generated, and subsequently reinforced, through membership). There is, third, the component of *consensus*, referring descriptively to the extent to which various sentiments and ideas are in fact common to participants. In addition, there are the contents of normative consensus, which may be described in many ways. This aspect gives rise actually to its own set of dimensions and to more or less systematic classificatory schemes, such as "the pattern variables" (Parsons, 1951); here, however, the principal property of interest is simply the "scope" of consensus, by which is meant the range of different activities, sentiments, etc., that are normatively regulated or defined.

reinforcement. It is assumed, in other words, that groups exhibit what Durkheim designated as an inherent tendency toward anomie (Durkheim, 1951).

"Interaction" refers to the observable actions of participants toward one another, or in response to one another, which occur in the course of their carrying on various activities jointly. Presumably the actions are motivated, guided by norms, and symbolically meaningful to participants. But the concept refers mainly to behavioral patterns and can be used without implying specific subjective states or dispositions, specific norms, or specific cultural meanings. Generally, by "degree of interaction" is meant the frequency with which participants (in their capacities as group members) interact together, but several other group properties also refer to some dimension of interaction. Three used here at times are the "scope" or "range" of interaction (referring to the various kinds of activities which group members engage in jointly), the relative frequency of "set events" and "pair events" (Chapple and Arensberg, 1940), and, which is slightly different, the degree of "centralization" of a group's "network" of interaction (Bavelas, 1951). Each is discussed more fully later.

Behavioral conformity (interaction in accord with commonly held expectations) or "compliance" with norms, like its opposite, "deviance," is descriptive. It refers here to the degree of correspondence (or, for deviance, of divergence) between the participants' qualities or performances and the shared normative expectations. Compliance with a norm, it is assumed, has the effect of reinforcing the norm's place in consensus, and consequently compliance is considered to be both an important mode of exercising influence in a group and an important mechanism countering the strain toward anomie (an indication of this strain being provided by the incidence of deviance).

To designate the extent to which participants define themselves and are defined by others as a social unit, the term "collective identity" is used. The participants' definitions here usually constitute a sector of the group's consensus, and may include cognitive ideas about the group's existence (its phenom-enological reality), sentiments concerning its existence (soli-darity), and evaluations of it compared with other groups or against various standards (cohesion).

To these four criteria, two others may be added.

One is the degree of visibility which participants have of the group's norms and of the correlative qualities and behaviors. Increasingly, visibility, or its counterpart at the status level, observability, has been recognized as a critical feature of groups, having been used, for example, as a condition of their formation (Michels, 1926; Lazarsfeld and Merton, 1954; Cohen, 1955—to mention a few) and as a condition of their effective functioning (Barnard, 1938). Since it plays a central role in this analysis and is therefore dealt with at length below, I will not discuss it further at this point.

The other criterion is implicit in Merton's formulation. It is an elementary feature of social situations that in the course of interacting, people evaluate one another in the light of the expectations they hold. They weigh each other's qualities and performances and, as it were, assign each one's participation a relative value that becomes in time, through a process of gen-eralization, an evaluation of the participant. To the extent that the standards used are commonly held and differences in observa-bility are not very great, there will be consensus among partici-pants on the ranks accorded one another. The degree to which there exists among a set of people a consistent, more or less stable set of rankings (loosely, a "stratification") has beeen used by Sherif among others to distinguish between groups and ag-gregates (Sherif and Sherif, 1956, pp. 126 *et passim*), and is a sixth criterion used here to define the existence of a group.

One set of people may thus be, so to speak, "less" of a group than another because among them the degree or range of shared expectations, frequency of interaction, compliance with group norms, sense of collective identity, level of visibility, or stability of rankings is less. But, and this is the important point here, there is for each criterion some minimum below which a set of people does not qualify as a sociological group. Some minimum of consensus, some minimum of interaction, some minimum of compliance, etc., are all required if a set of people is to constitute a group in the sociological sense. The cutting-points on each vary with the measures actually used, and they remain to be standardized, but the idea of such points is common to all sociological discussions of groups.[2]

Small Group

The propositions of the theory developed here are weighed against observations made on certain kinds of groups, namely small groups, and in turn the kinds of events the theory is used to explain are events in small groups. The propositions may have a wider applicability, but that is not claimed in these pages. Accordingly, a few comments need to be made about the concept of a "small" group.

Despite the name, such a group is not theoretically distinctive simply because it is small in size, and in consequence investigators have advanced a variety of other criteria for distinguishing the small group from other kinds. I shall not review these here, however, but merely state the three distinguishing features that define the term *small group* in this essay.

One of the three is that small groups exhibit, in comparison with others, a rather high degree of visibility. As defined by Merton, visibility refers to:

> . . . the extent to which the structure of a social organization provides occasion to those variously located in that structure to perceive the norms obtaining in the organization and the character of role-performance by those manning the organization. (Merton, 1957, p. 350)

A "small" group may be defined in part, then, as one in which the states of normative consensus and of compliance with the

---

[2] In terms of social-systems theory, the minimum points on these criteria constitute a set of "functional requirements" or "boundary conditions."

norms (behavioral conformity) are highly visible to all or most participants. Or, more exactly, it is one in which all or most participants have opportunities to observe whether and to what extent each of the others seems to accept the group norms in principle and to comply with them in fact. In Bales's phrasing:

> A small group is defined as any number of persons engaged in interaction with one another in a single face-to-face meeting or a series of such meetings, in which *each member receives some impression or perception of each other member* distinct enough so that he can . . . give some reaction (when questioned) to each of the others as an individual person . . . A number of persons who may be physically present at the same event (such as a lecture) but do not interact with one another enough for *each to be able to form any distinct impression of every other* . . . do not constitute a small group in the present sense (Bales, 1953, p. 30; emphasis added).

A similar but more conscious use of the term and concept occurs in a paper by Zetterberg:

> As a term denoting one kind of contact we shall choose *social visibility*. Social visibility is the probability that one actor has cognitions of action by (an) other actor(s) . . . When conditions of high social visibility exist we might speak of an *action system*. A set of actions is an action system, if and only if, all actors have high visibility of these actions . . . An informal luncheon discussion is an action system: each participant knows what views the others advance (Zetterberg, 1957, p. 183)[3].

There is, I might note, no assumption here that participants observe events and conditions in the group with equal accuracy. The point is merely that in small groups, in contrast to others, the structurally given opportunities for observing these matters are much more equally distributed among participants and the

---

[3] Zetterberg introduces the concept in part in order to distinguish between "action system" and "group," the former being in his usage a simpler kind of social system.

average level of visibility is much higher. Considerable differences in observability within a small group (i.e., over its members) are quite consistent with the statement that the small group differs from the large one by, among other things, a relatively high degree of the group property, visibility. And as the later analysis shows, sizable differences in observability among the members of a small group are in fact to be found.

A second distinguishing characteristic of "small" groups is the absence of stable, well-defined subgroups. A persistent connotation of the term has been that a small group is an elementary unit or collectivity in the sense of being the smallest social unit which is marked by collective identity or in which individuals think of themselves as having "membership." Implicit in this formulation is the idea that in a small group, still smaller ones (using the criteria of group set forth earlier) are not stable features. Since almost any group can be analyzed into a central or core subgroup and a set of peripheral members, the identifying feature of small groups is the absence, not of any, but of two or more stable, well-defined subgroups.

This criterion is not intended to rule out groups exhibiting coalitions, temporary factions, and the like. Nor is it intended to rule out groups whose participants are in other contexts related to one another, which may or may not be important. (Pairs of participants, for example, may be friends independently of their membership in a group under study, but whether the pairs constitute subgroups of that group is a question of fact, to be answered separately for each case, and cannot be decided in advance by a general rule.) What the criterion is intended to rule out is a group which typically operates in the form of multiple subgroups, however small it may be in size and whatever the degree of visibility it affords its participants. A research team, for example, consisting of three three-man units, each studying a sub-part of the project's topic, would not here be considered a small group if the participants usually interacted within their working units instead of regularly meeting as a group and thought of themselves as "in" one or another unit but only "on" the project. Similarly, a teen-age party in which the participants paired off early, forming fairly stable couples for the balance of the evening, would not be thought of as a small group. In both of these examples, the group in question is easily analyzed into constituent subgroups, each of which in turn qualifies as a group. For present purposes, groups divisible into such subgroups are not included in what is meant here by a small group.[4]

A third feature of the small group is partly implied in the other two but for our purposes should be mentioned explicitly. This is the degree to which the interaction takes place when all or most members are present and participating in a common activity—that is, the *frequency of interaction in "set events"* (Chapple and Arensberg, 1940; Whyte, 1943).[5] Ordinarily the level of visibility in a group is higher, the more the interaction among participants is restricted to such occasions (as opposed to occasions when interaction is carried on in subsets of pairs, triads, etc.), for it is through engaging in face-to-face interaction of this collective sort that any one participant is most likely to observe and to know accurately about any particular event or condition in the group. Similarly, subgroups (as opposed to coalitions, etc.) are less likely to develop, the more group interaction assumes this form. We may add to these two, then, the additional criterion that the interaction among the participants of a small group more often than not assumes the form of set events.

----

[4] In some cases a group may meet at times as a single unit and at other times in the form of subgroups. Sometimes it is useful to conceive of the subgroups not as constituents of the original group but as parts of its environment, in which case the original group is viewed as a group during its unity phases only. Such a procedure, though, merely shifts the problem around, for it then becomes necessary to show that what remains as the (small) group is sufficiently independent of its environment to constitute an instance of a relatively closed system. Clearly, if all variations of interest within the unity phases are determined by variations occurring during the subgroup phases, little would be gained by employing this procedure.

[5] This usage of "set event" departs slightly from its original definition.

The Status of Member

In examining the internal structure of small groups the most useful entity to employ for most purposes is the status (or role) of member.[6] Like any social status this entity is both something less and something more than the person of an individual participant.

It is something less because membership in a small group almost always engages but a segment of a person. In most small groups some members are more engaged than others, and some small groups typically engage more of their members than other groups do, but all small groups probably leave out some part of

[6] As noted above, Parsons (1951, p. 25) makes this point for the analysis of social systems generally.

It is not necessary for an analyst to use role or status as his theoretical unit when examining small groups, however. "Actions" may be used, as Parsons comments, and as the work of Bales and of Lennard and Bernstein (1960) shows. Homans (1950), on the other hand, begins his analysis of "the human group" with the role-relation as his main unit, the propositions being of the order, "In any role-relation of a small group, the higher the rate of task interaction, the greater the feelings of mutual liking." Only later, when he begins to discuss leadership, does he shift units, substituting status for role-relation. His propositions at this later point are thus of the order, "For any member of a small group, the wider the range of others with whom he interacts and the more frequently he interacts with them, the higher his rank." (These are not Homans' propositions exactly, but only similar to two of his.)

It might seem that anything phrased in terms of status or role can be phrased in terms of role-relations, and vice-versa. But the implicit transformations are by no means simple. In the case of Homans' theory, for example, his two sets of propositions, the one about role-relations and the other about statuses, describe two rather different structural patterns. This is not the place to go into the matter, and so I will only say here that (1) his propositions about role-relations assume a structure wherein interaction between any two members is greater the smaller the difference in their ranks, but that (2) his propositions about leadership assume a structure wherein the frequency with which any one member interacts with any other varies directly with the second's rank. These are, obviously, different types of structures. They are not necessarily mutually exclusive—a group could alternate between them by changing from one to the other and back again—but propositions that are true for one are not necessarily true for the other. For further discussion of this point, see below, pp. 112-117. Since this note was originally written, Homans has himself taken note of the difficulty (Homans, 1961, ch. 10).

the person of a participant, and usually a fairly large part. What is left out, the "rest of the person," is always causally relevant to the member's status-behaviors and is thus causally relevant to the functioning of the group. But, as was said earlier, it forms not a part of the group proper but a part of its psychological environment.

Membership is something more than the person also. It includes not only the activities that in a behavioral sense seem to be the participant's, but also the morally binding expectations that define what members should do or be like and what they should think, feel, and value. Since these are commonly or collectively held and form an integral part of the group's state of normative consensus, they give to the concept of membership a decidedly collective character.

The use of the term *status* requires comment. One could follow Linton (1936, ch. 8) and designate the fact of membership and the obligations and rights consequent upon that fact— the "morally binding" expectations—by the term *status*, and the activities of a participant in response to the obligations and in exercise of the rights by the term *role*. This distinction between status and role, however, has become blurred in recent writings and, hence, so too has the broader distinction between expectations and behaviors which it reflects. Two examples may illustrate the point. Parsons, although following Linton closely when he introduces the two terms (Parsons, 1951, p. 25), subsequently says of a role that it is a set of expectations, that it "is a sector of the total orientation system of an individual actor . . ." (*Ibid.*, p. 38). And many writers have used *role* to refer to a subset of a status' expectations (composed of those defining its relations with a particular other status) and *role-conflict* to refer to a situation where one subset contradicts a second (composed of those defining its relations with a second other status).

The distinction between expectations and behavior, however, is a critical one—the difference between manifest and latent functions, for instance, largely turns on it. Since new terms are emerging that keep the distinction salient, terms such as role-performance or status-behavior, role-expectation or status-obligation, I shall follow the newer conventions and speak of "status" (or "role") when both the typical behaviors and the usual expectations constitutive of "membership" are referred to and "status-behavior" or "status-expectation" when only one or the other is meant.[7]

Besides being the unit of group, the status of member is also the unit to which the exercise of influence and the other properties are attributed. No other distinctions are made, however, the status itself being left unanalyzed in almost all cases. Neither the particular expectations and behaviors that constitute the status of member in specific groups (such as an American middle-class family or a university seminar), nor the kinds of expectations and behaviors that distinguish membership in one kind of group (e.g., expressive or intimate groups) from membership in another kind (e.g., instrumental groups), concern us here. For present purposes all small groups and all membership statuses in such groups are treated as if they were alike, however much they in fact differ. Army squads, baseball teams, sewing clubs, and farm families, if small groups as defined above, are all viewed as "basically alike."

[7] To determine whether, in a particular situation, we have to do with phenomena that may be conceived in terms of roles and statuses, two separable aspects or dimensions need to be examined: the degree of consensus among a set of people on what is expected of a role- or status-occupant, and the degree of uniformity or similarity in the behavior of those so designated. A role or status may thus be more or less clearly "defined" (referring to expectations) and more or less clearly "patterned" (referring to behaviors). Presumably sets of activities, to warrant being designated as instances of roles or statuses, must exhibit some minimum of definition and patterning. It is striking that despite the fundamental nature of these concepts practically no systematic work on their measurement has been done, with the result that at present it is an entirely open question just how well defined and clearly patterned the activities must be. (But see Nadel, 1957, and Goode, 1960.) This question need not be dealt with here, though, since if a set of people constitute a group as defined above, it follows from the criteria used (particularly consensus and compliance) that the membership activities are sufficiently defined and patterned to constitute a status.

Similarly, within groups as well, the distinctive roles are treated as if they were alike, however much they may in fact be differentiated, and members are thus viewed as "basically alike" even though in point of fact their status-definitions and corresponding status-behaviors may be highly differentiated.

This procedure is followed because, as was said in the Introduction, the task for the greater part of the book is to identify and examine a process that presumably operates in every group, whatever its institutional form and whatever its degree of role differentiation. Differences among groups with respect to both their institutional forms and their complement of differentiated roles do of course enter the analysis eventually, but they do so only toward the end, where their effects on the operation of the basic process are examined.

The Interaction System of a Group

The six criteria listed at the beginning of this chapter serve, as descriptive concepts, to identify sets of people constituting sociological groups. They also describe the particular features of groups that most interest us here. It was said in the Introduction that for the purposes of this study it is desirable to circumscribe rather narrowly what is considered to be "in" a group, viewed as an interaction system, and to locate in the "environment" of the system a number of features of groups, or of their participants, that for other purposes one might view as in the system. In order to provide the conceptual background for the selection of the determinants of influence and for the later discussion of the effects on influence of various "external" factors, a brief sketch is given here of the relationships among the group properties and between this narrowly delimited interaction system of a group and various causally relevant external factors. It need hardly be emphasized that the sketch is no more than that, that it is not a statement of a systematic theory but only an attempt to depict in a general way what for the purposes of this analysis are thought of as the principal elements of a group's interaction system.

The two planes of normative consensus and interaction, and the relations between them, contain the core phenomena of interest to us. On the one hand, the interactions among participants are guided or regulated by the shared norms and, on the other, it is through the interaction sequences that normative consensus is maintained. As was mentioned, consensus is not assumed to be a stable, given condition but to fluctuate in degree, content, scope, and so on, and, in particular, to be subject to an inherent tendency toward anomie. The principal mechanism blocking the working out of this tendency is compliance, or interaction in accordance with existing or evolving norms. More generally, since such effects indicate the exercise of influence as defined above, it is assumed that interaction continually reacts back on and influences the norms that guide it and that in consequence the contents of consensus are continually being either reinforced or, as is more likely, modified in one respect or another.

The generally, but not invariably, positive effects of interaction on consensus are owing presumably to two intervening, simultaneous mechanisms. One links interaction to the visibility of norms and thence to subjective conformity (the degree of congruence between the norms to which any participant is in fact committed and the norms to which he is expected within the group to be committed). Presumably, the more frequently the members of a group interact, the more visible to each are the expectations they in fact share or expect one another to share; and the more the members are aware of what is normative in the group, the more the actions of each are likely to be oriented to or guided by norms that are in fact shared.

The other mechanism links interaction to the visibility of performances and qualities, the evaluations by others, and the subjective states of felt-belonging and motivation to participate. Provided their compliance is visible, the more members comply with the norms, the more likely they are to be positively evaluated or sanctioned; and the more they are positively sanctioned, the greater their sense of collective identity or felt-belonging, which in turn, it may be assumed, is positively related to the cohesion of the group and to the members' motivation to participate. (The motivation itself, however, lies "outside" the interaction system.)

These basic phenomena of groups, which for present purposes constitute the core of their interaction systems, take place in a context composed of several environments, each of which is the locus of various factors that are causally relevant to the phenomena. Four broad kinds of environments (or classes of causally relevant external factors) may be distinguished. In many ways the most important, particularly for a small group, is its psychological environment, which is composed of those sectors of each participant's personality system which are not directly engaged in the membership status. There is also the group's social environment, composed of other groups and more complex structures; its physical and biological environment; and its cultural environment, since most groups do not invent their institutional form or evolve the contents of their consensus but receive them, as it were, from the larger culture.

The nature and degree of dependence of a group's interaction system on factors in any one of these environments varies from group to group and environment to environment. But every interaction system can be assumed to be dependent to some extent on each sort of factor, and variations in these external factors can be assumed to occasion some degree of variation in the elements within the system.[8] One line of dependence of an

---

[8] Several ways exist to formulate these relations between a system and its environment(s), but for present purposes it is enough to assume that only certain ranges of variation in the system-states (here, interaction, consensus, etc.) are tolerable, that these ranges define the boundary conditions or functional requirements of the system, and that certain environmental conditions are necessary if the boundaries are to be maintained or the functional requirements met.

Since for a set of people to constitute a group there must be a certain

interaction system on its environment is through its reliance on the presence of relevant norms in the personality systems of participants, since a minimum of normative consensus depends (by definition) on the participants' being minimally committed to the norms in question. Interaction can and usually does affect the normative commitments of participants, but the "holding" of internalized norms is a psychological state and internalization is a psychological process. "Normative commitment" of participants thus designates an important factor in the psychological environment of an interaction system.

Given a requisite degree of normative commitment, the motivation to comply with norms can to a large extent be taken for granted, but the motivation to do so through participating *in the particular group* cannot be. This motivational commitment to the particular group as opposed to other groups, on which the sheer occurrence of interaction depends, is partly caught by the concept of collective identity, but it is more commonly referred to merely as "cohesion." Interaction can and usually does affect the motivational balance of participants, but the balance itself and the correlative motivational processes are located in the personality systems of the participants, not in the interaction system of the group. This link between interaction and the motivations it requires, or "cohesion," is then another important line of dependence between the system and its psychological environment.

Normative commitment and cohesion may be necessary conditions of compliance, but they are seldom sufficient conditions as well, as the frequency with which intentions and consequences fail to coincide would suggest. In addition, the mini-

---

minimum of each of the six properties, these minima may be taken as a set of boundary conditions for the interaction system of a group. Thus, if there is "too little" consensus, interaction, visibility, etc., the set of people no longer constitutes a group for sociological purposes. Moreover, because the people are to constitute a small group, certain additional limits are imposed on the ranges of variation which the properties may exhibit. There are probably certain maxima, as well as minima, defining the tolerable variations, but these may be ignored for present purposes.

mum of compliance, or more generally, of influence, requires the presence in one or more of the environments of various "facilitating conditions." In a rapid, abstract sketch such as this one, the broad category of facilitating conditions must remain rather general, but it refers, for example, to the performance capabilities of members, the availability of "expected" or socially necessary physical objects or conditions, the performance of various actions by non-members, the existence in the larger culture of various techniques, kinds of information, and so forth. If a group is conceived to be an acting agent, the relevant means, goals, and conditions are usually conceived to lie in one or another of its environments, and would here come under the heading of facilitating conditions. The term "adaptation" may be used to designate the boundary relations between these conditions and the states internal to the interaction system of a group.

This very general listing will be sufficient for our purposes, since the point of these last remarks is merely to provide a basis for discussing the impact on the exercise of influence of various factors that are not conceived to be within a group's interaction system. The other defining properties of this system, visibility and ranking, while directly dependent in particular circumstances on environmental conditions, can for the present be treated as internal states whose dependence on external factors is in general mediated by their relations with the other three internal states, interaction, consensus, and influence.

These five internal states are the principal ones of interest here. Others of course could be added, such as degree of role differentiation, relative balance between expressive and instrumental activities, goal attainment or effectiveness, and so forth. I choose not to add them because, though they seem in general no less basic than the others, their relevance specifically to the distribution of influence can be more satisfactorily traced by introducing them at a later point in the analysis.

Four Properties of the Status of Member

The properties predicated of the status of member derive directly from these internal states of a group's interaction system. They are obtained simply by considering the differences among the members of a group with respect to each. Just as interaction systems may differ with respect to their rank structure, frequency of interaction, and so forth, so may participants within a given interaction system differ from one another in analogous respects. Thus:

Group Property	Status Property
Rank structure	Rank
Frequency of interaction	Centrality
Level of visibility	Observability
Degree of normative consensus	(Subjective) Conformity
Amount of influence exercised	Influence

Each of these status properties is now discussed.

Rank

Rank is defined here phenomenologically, as referring to the generally agreed upon worth or standing of a member relative to the other members. Because neither the content of normative standards nor the extent of role differentiation is taken into account at this point, the source or basis of a member's relative rank is in principle irrelevant. In particular, it makes no difference that in one group the members' relative ranks derive from institutionalized evaluations of well-defined, stably allocated statuses (professor and student in a seminar, father and child in a family), whereas in another group, whose members are formally equal, the rank differences derive from differential evaluations of qualities or performances (high- and low-ranking participants in an orals study group). The propositions containing the concept rank apply equally well in principle to both kinds of groups.

In both, also, marginal situations may occur that make it difficult to gauge the relative ranks of members. Where well-defined ranks attach to statuses, performance evaluations of personnel may be so at variance with their status-derived ranks that the ranks of the members are in fact indeterminate, being arranged in one order according to one criterion and in an entirely different order by the other. Where members are formal equals, there may be no consensus on relative standing (or there may be consensus on each of several criteria but not on an over-all, general standing or value to the group), in which case, again, the ranks of the members are in fact indeterminate But such situations are probably infrequent, and short-lived when they occur; relatively distinct rank differences are probably present in most groups most of the time.

The particular way rank is measured must of course be adjusted to fit the circumstances. In groups where rank differences exist among well-defined, stably allocated statuses, each member's relative rank can be inferred from the generally acknowledged rank of the status he occupies (qualified if necessary by his evaluated fitness to occupy it). An in-between measurement situation occurs in groups having differentially ranked but not stably allocated statuses, for example, teams with a rotating captaincy or committees with rotating offices. In such groups the members' ranks are probably best indicated jointly by the rank(s) of the status(es) and the agreed-upon suitability of each to occupy the status(es). Finally, in groups lacking well-defined differentiated statuses, the members' ranks are indicated by the ratings they give each other in response to questions that do not specify particular performances or qualities ("personally likable") but ask vaguely about "importance to the group," "outstanding" or "undesirable" members, "contribution to the group," perhaps "leadership," and so forth.

Some groups of formal equals may be "groups" only marginally by the criterion of stable rankings, in which case such ratings may not indicate ranks exactly but something short of that. They may reflect evaluations of particular actions or qualities that have not (yet) been generalized to the point of constituting ranks of members. The "approvals" so measured may be parts of the process whereby stable and generalized ranks are formed, but they are quite different both from ranks proper and from the kinds of specific approvals that are given once ranks come into existence. They thus probably indicate some sort of "proto-rank" and need to be interpreted accordingly.

Centrality

Centrality[9] designates how close a member is to the "center" of the group's interaction network and thus refers simultaneously to the frequency with which a member participates in interaction with other members and the number or range of other members with whom he interacts. Like the corresponding group property of interaction, centrality is a behavioral concept and is indicated by observations of overtly visible patterns of actions. The extent to which a member is "at the center of attention," in the sense that others are concerned about him or about his reactions to them, or that they intend their actions to be noticed (or not noticed) by him, is irrelevant to his centrality.

Although not new, the concept has attracted considerable attention in recent years because of its role in studies of the communications networks of complex organizations. Usually such networks are conceived to be in the shape of wheels lying flat: The hub of the wheel forms an information center; tactical information (in the form of "field reports") flows from the units at the organization's outer rim along the spokes and to the hub; strategic information (in the form of "orders") flows from the hub along the spokes and to the units operating at the rim. This horizontal picture of an organization is specifically intended to contrast with the vertical picture of an organization as a pyramid or hierarchy. Similarly, the centrality of a position in the organization's communications system is intended to be logically inde-

[9] The principal works in which the concept occurs in one form or another and from which it derives are: Barnard (1938, 1946), Bavelas (1951), Leavitt (1951), Lewin (1950), Merton (1957, ch. 9), and Feld (1959).

pendent of its rank in the organization's hierarchy. In point of fact, of course, the two properties, rank and centrality, usually are related, but the relationship is a matter of fact, not a consequence of the definitions of the concepts.

The centralization of a group's network of interaction contains two dimensions, and so, therefore, does centrality as a role property. A network is more or less centralized depending upon differences among members in (a) the number of others with whom each interacts and (b) the frequency with which each interacts within the group. The two tend to be highly correlated, and a composite score is thus ordinarily unnecessary in order to gauge each member's relative centrality. One can imagine situations where they would not be correlated, though, and for these some index combining the two would have to be devised.

A fairly wide variety of measures may be used to indicate one or the other aspect of centrality, but some are more reliable or valid than others. The Appendix to this chapter therefore contains a brief critical review of the more common methods. Perhaps the only point to repeat here is that in using interaction rates from who-to-whom matrices, I consider every act in which a member figures—whether as communicator, specific recipient, or one recipient among several—as instancing an interaction of his. He *acts* differently, of course, depending upon the part he plays, but he *interacts* in all three cases.

Observability

Visibility, as defined above in the quotation from Merton, refers to a structural property of groups in virtue of which participants are more or less able to observe the actual norms in the group, and the actual role-qualities and role-behaviors of participants. Here, however, differences among the members of a given group concern us, not differences among groups. A group's structure usually gives some members more and better opportunities to observe the events and conditions in the group than it does other members. Statuses thus differ in the observability they afford their occupants, much as groups differ in the visibility they afford their members. Although analogous, the concepts are not the same, and it is useful to distinguish them by letting observability refer to the status property and visibility to the group property.

Like the other concepts used here, observability, in one form or another, has been in use for a long time, particularly in analyses of authority structures. That leaders lead in virtue of their followers' attitudes, and the inference from this, that they must keep in touch with the attitudes and opinions on which their leadership rests, are hardly ideas of recent origin.

> . . . As force is always on the side of the governed, the governors have nothing to support them but opinion. It is, therefore, on opinion only that government is founded. . . . The soldan of Egypt or the emperor of Rome might drive his harmless subjects like brute beasts against their sentiments and inclination. But he must, at least, have led his *mamelukes* or *praetorian bands*, like men, by their opinion (David Hume, *Of the First Principles of Government*).

What is recent, it would seem, is that the idea of "keeping in touch" has come to play a more central and explicit role not only in theories of authority but also in theories of influence. For this development, the writings of Barnard are probably most responsible. On the one hand, he held that "whatever the nature of authority, it is inherent in the simple organization unit" (1938, p. 161), and, on the other, that "objective authority is only maintained if the positions [of authority] or leaders continue to be adequately informed" (*ibid.*, p. 174). He was thus led to examine the structure of small groups for features and problems that are commonly thought to exist only in large ones and to suggest, among other things, that "keeping in touch" is no less important for a factory supervisor than for an Egyptian soldan.

In using the concept of observability here, I shall not pay systematic attention to observability of role-performances (or role-qualities) because it raises both theoretical and methodological issues distinctly different from those raised by observability of norms. Also, the working definition of a concept that entails a notion of potentiality or capacity is complicated at best, and involves questions of a methodological nature that cannot be satisfactorily handled here. I shall therefore construe observability (of norms) as referring in practice to a member's actual knowledge of group norms, and not attempt to assess his structurally given opportunity to know them.

In principle, the measurement of observability in this restricted sense presents few difficulties. One uses the "opinion-estimate" technique and asks each member to estimate how many in the group would agree or disagree with each of a number of statements. At the same time, each respondent checks off how he himself feels about each statement, and this latter set of responses, summed for the membership as a whole, provides the observer's estimate of group opinion. Each member's estimate of group opinion is then compared with the observer's estimate, a member's degree of observability being indicated by the degree of fit between his estimate and the observer's.

In practice, however, there are several difficulties. Some arise in connection with measuring normative consensus which is discussed in the Appendix to the chapter. Some relate specifically to the measurement of observability of norms and are discussed in the next chapter, when several relevant studies are reviewed.

Conformity

Conformity may be defined as the condition (or degree) of congruence between a member's profile on the relevant norms and the profile of group-held norms. It does *not* refer to the congruence between his behavior and group norms, which is compliance and plays an entirely distinct role in the theory.

The measurement of conformity, like that of visibility, is simple in principle. Usually the observer develops a set of statements which he thinks may reflect the normative and near-normative elements in a group's working consensus, has each member indicate his feelings about each statement, and then compares the feelings each has expressed with the group's views, which are usually indicated for these purposes by an unweighted aggregation of the individual members' responses. The comparison of each member's views with the presumed views of the group is unobjectionable. The measurement of a group's normative consensus, however, is more complicated than is usually recognized, and the validity of most procedures leaves much to be desired, as the discussion in the Appendix to the chapter suggests.

One point requiring comment here is the occasional use of the term to refer to a member's *becoming* more conforming than he was, usually in regard to some one *particular* group judgment or standard. For this sort of process I shall use the term *convergence* and for the condition it results in, the term *acceptance*, simply because congruence in one selected respect is so much narrower in scope than the concept of conformity as that is used here. Owing to this difference in scope, indicators of acceptance (e.g., a subject's agreeing in private with a previously reached group decision) have low validity as indicators of conformity; but I shall nevertheless use them in this way, in the absence of better data.[10] Indicators of convergence (e.g., the percentage decrease over time in the variation within a set of perceptual judgments) cannot be used, because how much a person changes bears no necessary relation to how congruent his views are with group opinion compared to how congruent other members' views are.

The Concept of Influence

Influence was defined earlier as the effects of action on the group's normative consensus. A member's influence, over a given period of time, thus consists of the impact of his actions on consensus

[10] See Zetterberg (1963, pp. 44-48) for a careful discussion of internal validity in terms of "scope of content."

during that period; and his relative influence, which is what mainly interests us, is the impact of his actions relative to the impact of the other members' actions.

These further comments on the concept concern normative consensus and the tendency to anomie; influence as a mechanism countering the tendency, and various kinds of influential actions; the measurement of influence; and the relations between this concept of influence and the concept of personal influence.

Normative Consensus and the Tendency to Anomie

The normative consensus of a group, as defined earlier, refers to a set of ideas and sentiments. The members are motivationally and morally committed to these ideas and sentiments, in the sense that each feels they should inform his and the others' actions in the group. And the members share or hold them in common, in the sense that they respond to or sanction one another in terms of the ideas and sentiments, the sanctions being positive for actions visibly in accord with or expressing the ideas and sentiments and negative for actions visibly contravening or failing to express them. This normative consensus is conceived to be the actual or working consensus of a group, not what the members or others think ought to be the normative ideas and sentiments.

By assumption, this consensus is not a stable or constant state. Rather, it is assumed that it tends to disintegrate, that in groups generally, there is at work a tendency to anomie. The norms of a group, it is true, are to some extent anchored in the personalities of the participants (by definition) and thus to some extent their adherence to them may be counted upon. But at the same time, each person is a member of several groups, and there is little reason to assume that the norms of different groups are in general mutually reinforcing. Indeed, it is probably more often the opposite, so that for any one group the other memberships of its participants, and their other commitments, contribute indirectly to its tendency toward a state of anomie.

Within any one group, then, it can be assumed that no member fully conforms subjectively to the group's norms. Not only is each likely to lack a moral or motivational commitment to at least some of the ideas or sentiments that are normative for most. But, in addition, the salience of the commitments to any one member as an individual is almost always lower on the average than is their salience to the members collectively. Even if, in Durkheim's phrase, a group were "a perfect cloister of exemplary individuals," and all members "held" the requisite normative ideas and sentiments, there is every reason to suppose that the norms would become progressively less salient as commitments, and progressively less effective as guides to action, in the absence of recurrent situations which call for their use and expression and which thereby reinforce their place in each member's hierarchy of commitments.

The tendency toward anomie is of course just that, a tendency. Few groups ever reach the state, since before anomie becomes generalized the members' motivations have in most groups probably fallen below the minimum needed to sustain interaction. Nevertheless, it is useful to conceive of such a tendency as operative in groups; and to conceive of behavioral divergence from actual norms as indicative of the tendency. Most groups can presumably tolerate some degree of deviance —indeed, as Durkheim has suggested, some degree of it should be considered "normal" (1950, pp. 65-73). But in most, the extent to which the activities of the participants can depart from the norms without occasioning any basic changes in the structure of the group is probably not very great. For once the mechanisms checking the anomic tendency fail to operate satisfactorily and the tendency gains momentum, a degenerative cycle sets in, whereby the levels of cohesion and consensus drop, causing in turn a drop in the frequency of interaction, which brings about a further drop in cohesion and consensus, and so forth (see Homans, 1950, esp. ch. 13).

Some Varieties of Influential Actions

The principal mechanism checking the tendency to anomie, or so overcoming it that a developmental cycle occurs, is the exercise of influence. It performs this function in several ways or, alternatively, there are several kinds of influential actions. The most basic probably is behavioral conformity, the effect of which is to reinforce or keep salient the norm complied with. Not quite the same in substance although similar in effect are explicit sanctions (or the explicit interpretation of events as sanctions), whereby positive rewards are associated with behavioral conformity and punishments with behavioral deviance.

The degree of normative consensus may be maintained not only by keeping its contents intact, so to speak, but also by altering them to keep up with the changes which situational factors are causing in the group's range of activities. Any group operates in a complex environment of varying stimuli which require definition and action, and new forms of behavior by group members may develop in response to changes in the stimuli. These are nonconforming behaviors, but they are not necessarily deviant: They may fail to be conforming not because they contravene a norm but because there is (as yet) no norm pertaining to them. Actions on consensus that extend it to cover previously undefined situations constitute another kind of influence.

Deviant behavior disturbs consensus, and in that sense affects it. It is not, however, an exercise of influence, although ordinarily it is associated with the exercise of influence. Deviant behavior does not directly alter the state of consensus but, insofar as it is visible, it brings into question the status of the idea or sentiment departed from. Is the idea or sentiment, a part of the normative consensus, as was supposed, or is it not? The answer to the question is given by the strength of the reaction to the deviance. A strong condemnation of the departure counters directly the anomic tendency which the deviance reflects; on the other hand, continuous tolerance of deviance would certainly have to be taken as indicating anomic tendencies so far as the particular ideas or sentiments are concerned.

Deviance that is concentrated on particular ideas or sentiments, however, may indicate not that anomic tendencies are generally on the increase within the group, but merely that a redefinition of the corresponding activities is occurring. The incidence of the deviance indicates that previously prevailing sentiments or ideas no longer prevail, that they are no longer normative. At a certain point, therefore, if the activities continue to occur in their deviant form, they no longer instance deviant behavior but only behavior that is not normatively defined. The activities fall outside the ranges of explicitly proscribed, permitted, and prescribed behaviors and into the range of undefined behaviors. At this point, if influence is exercised to extend consensus to cover the activity, it again becomes normatively defined; only the norms are different. Looked at in terms of the whole sequence of changes, the initial deviance, although not the immediate cause of the new norm, was certainly its precursor and probably a condition of its introduction. As Durkheim says of crime, so one might also say of deviance generally: "How many times, indeed, it is only an anticipation of future morality—a step toward what it will be!" (1950, p. 71).

A somewhat different way to picture influence as effects on consensus is to start from an ordering of the ideas and sentiments that prevail in a group at a given time. Some of the ideas and sentiments will be defined as normative, some will be nearly normative, and some will be well outside the normative sphere; and within the normative sector, some will be prescribed, some permitted, and some proscribed.

Over time, it may be assumed, owing to situational changes of both a random and a systematic sort, the content of group opinion will fluctuate. In the short run, sentiments and ideas will shift positions, some becoming more salient and some less, some more normative, some less. In the long run, in the absence of counteracting mechanisms, group opinion will become disorganized. The boundaries separating the normative from the

non-normative and the prescribed from the permissible and proscribed will disappear. And the ideas and sentiments will no
longer be a part of group opinion but merely the ideas and
sentiments of the particular individuals considered severally.

From this point of view, influence consists of stabilizing the
normative area of group opinion or of making *orderly* changes
in its boundaries or contents. An idea or sentiment that is
exemplified or explicitly supported by actions is, so to speak,
moved in the course of interaction toward the center or core
of consensus and toward being prescribed. One that is irrelevant
to the actually occurring interactions is, because it is not being
reinforced, moved away from the center, toward permissibility
and in time toward being non-normative. One that is contra-
vened by behavior is also moved away from the normative area
but more rapidly, as it were. And one that is explicitly opposed
is moved toward the normative area but as a proscribed idea or
sentiment.

This is perhaps a fanciful picturing of changes in the state of
consensus, but it is a useful one. Among other things, it allows
us to see that any single concrete interaction sequence is probably influential in several ways, since it probably has several
different kinds of effects. It is also the picturing that is most
directly relevant to measurement, since it suggests that even with
fairly arbitrary cutting points between the normative and the
non-normative, and between the prescribed, permitted, and
proscribed, one can chart empirically both the effects that come
from the exercise of influence and the slow disintegration of
consensus that reflects its absence.

Substantively, too, there may be many kinds of influence, since
ideas and sentiments may be classified by their content in
many different ways. Simply because it constitutes an important
but sometimes unnoticed substantive kind of influence, I mention here the exercise of influence regarding the positions and
ranks of members. Ideas and sentiments about who should and
should not be a member, who should play one or another role,
and who should have one or another rank, are obviously of

continuing critical importance in the day-to-day operation of a group, and so identifying those who exert a disproportionate influence on these ideas and sentiments is probably equivalent, in most cases, to identifying the key personnel in a group so far as the exercise of influence is concerned.

The Measurement of Influence

The measurement of this conception of influence presents several problems. Starting from the imagery in the preceding paragraphs, it would probably be possible to design a procedure that would give fairly valid estimates of the relative degree of influence of the different members of a group. In outline, measurements of group opinion would be needed at two (or more) points in time, and observations would have to be made of the activities of participants in the intervening period. From such information, degrees of influence could be attributed to the participants, according to the observed changes in group opinion, the ideas and sentiments each held, and the ideas and sentiments each exemplified or expressed in his actions.

In none of the studies reviewed in subsequent chapters, however, is influence measured in this way. Further description of a valid procedure would thus be programmatic, suggesting how the concept should be defined in possible future researches, rather than pragmatic, suggesting how it can be defined for the purpose of analyzing existing findings, and I will therefore leave to a later study a full description of valid methods for measuring influence as defined here. Methodological comments on the various means of measuring influence now in use appear in the Appendix to this chapter.

Social Influence and Personal Influence

There is one more general point to make on the conception of influence that informs this study. In its most general sense, influence connotes phenomena that recur with great regularity in culturally and historically disparate settings. It thus touches on phenomena that are inherent in human interaction and that any picturing of an abstract, generalized "system of interaction" must deal with. Most current concepts of influence, however, by focusing almost entirely on the effects of one person's actions on the attitudes or behaviors of another person, draw attention away from the impact of participants' actions on the interaction system itself. Interaction is seen in these conceptions as a means of exercising influence, but it is not seen as itself influenced, as being continually shaped in turn by the influence that is exercised. Or rather, to be more exact—since "all interaction has an effect, however slight, upon behavior in the immediate situation" (Merton, 1957, p. 415, n. 20) —the influence that is exercised in the course of interaction is not seen as continually and systematically affecting the very framework of norms that constitutes the context of the interaction.

Such effects, it seems to me, are just as important theoretically as the effects of interaction on the attitudes and behaviors of specific persons, and some way of calling attention to them seems required. It should be possible to study influence as a process of the interaction system of a group without having to work with a concept that presents it basically as a process between two persons who may or may not be interacting in the context of a group. The conception outlined here is intended to meet this need and to facilitate this kind of analysis.

It is designed, of course, not as an all-purpose replacement for the concept of personal or interpersonal influence, as that concept is used, for example, in Katz and Lazarsfield (1955), but merely as an addition to it, as another way of thinking about the exercise of influence. This notion of what, for purposes of contrast, may be referred to as "social" influence, is intended, it is true, to draw attention away from the changes that interaction produces in persons, and to focus attention instead on the changes it produces in the structure and operation of groups. But since the concrete data to be examined are much the same whichever concept is used, the two conceptions imply not mutually exclusive but only alternative modes of analysis and interpretation.

Appendix to Chapter 2

Notes on the Measurement of Centrality, Normative Consensus, and Influence

CENTRALITY

A member of a group is more or less central within its interaction network depending upon the number of other members with whom he interacts and the frequency with which he interacts within the group. In most small groups, every member interacts with every other, and centrality is therefore measured in such groups by interaction rates. There are two general ways of obtaining these "rates," by directly observing the members and by asking them about their behavior.

As for the first, any observational method is satisfactory that requires the observer to score (1) *all* kinds of interactions in the period of observation, not just particular kinds, and (2) the recipients of acts as well as the originators. Care is needed, however, in inferring relative centrality from observational records.

Most scoring schemes use for their unit of observation not "an interaction" but "an act," which is usually scored as A-to-B (with or without a notation indicating the class of acts in which it falls, e.g., "gives opinion"). If interaction enters at all, it does so as an "exchange" of acts between two persons, its occurrence being marked by the action's changing hands. Roughly, then, "an interaction" is indicated by two scored acts in sequence, A-to-B plus B-to-A. The distinction between one person's originating an action toward another and the second's responding invariably involves this sort of scoring in sequence—first one and then the other acts. The concept of interaction, however, entails the notion of simultaneity. A may be observably acting toward B, but insofar as normal interaction is occurring, B, it must be assumed, is *simultaneously* (re)acting toward A. In fact, B's actions must be registering with A simultaneously with A's acting. "Normal interaction," in short, is the kind that takes place in face-to-face situations where feedback is concurrent with action.[1]

For this reason, it seems necessary to depart from common procedures and to interpret each scored act (in a face-to-face situation) as instancing "an interaction," which means that every act that is scored A-to-B is taken as implying an unscored act, B-to-A. Consequently, any act in which a member figures, whether he figures in it as communicator, specific recipient, or one recipient among several, instances an interaction of his. Of course, he *acts* differently depending upon whether he originates an action or responds to the action of another. The point here is only that he *interacts* in either case. To read a member's degree of centrality from a who-to-whom matrix, then, one sums in some fashion his acts initiated, acts received singly, and acts received as a member of "the group."

Since investigators do not always record both the communicators and the recipients of the scored acts, the question arises, How validly do records of only acts received or only acts initiated indicate the relative centrality of members of a group? Two points may be made in answer to this question. First, acts initiated can probably be scored far more reliably than acts received.[2] Second, if the question is interpreted as asking, When does the rank order of members that results from using both pieces of information not correspond to the rank order that results from using only one of them, Bales and his associates provide a partial answer. Some time ago they reported that over a large number of *ad hoc* discussion groups, several different pieces of information placed the participants in the same order:

> . . . If the participants in a small group are ranked by the total number of acts they initiate, they will also tend to be

[1] It is of course possible to prevent a continuous flow of response experimentally by using any of a number of devices which in daily life "substitute" for face-to-face interaction, devices such as telephone calls, written messages, and so forth. When this is done, or when the communications in a natural group often take these forms, observable events occur in a sequence that resembles the action-reaction model. But conceptually such "mechanically" mediated communications are not the characteristic form of interaction but a special form, namely, the form in which feedback is delayed. When the amount of delay in feedback reaches a certain (arbitrary) point, one presumably decides that "interaction" is not occurring, for example, when it reaches the point where the only communications between A and B are the messages A writes to B.

[2] For example, see Festinger and Hutte (1954, esp. pp. 515-516).

ranked: 1) by the number of acts they receive; 2) by the number of acts they address to specific other individuals; and 3) by the number of acts they address to the group as a whole (1951, p. 468).

From this it follows that the participants will also be ranked in the same order by the total number of interactions in which they take part at all. But, as the authors say, their "generalizations are average empirical tendencies" of the kinds of group they studied.

> Any specific group, or some particular types of groups, may present exceptions to the generalizations we describe, in one or more particulars, depending on the conditions operating. For example, we have often found particular exceptions to predicted rank positions in cases where one of the members disagrees with the others persistently, and so tends to attract or receive a disproportionate amount of communication. And we have also found exceptions when two highly interactive and agreeing members form a sub-group vis-à-vis a third neglected or rejected member (*ibid.*, pp. 467-468).

Consequently, where subgroupings seem to exist or where groups are coping with cases of extreme deviance, centrality is better gauged from observational records that include all relevant data.

A somewhat different limitation on the validity of partial interaction records is suggested by accounts of "traditional" groups.[3] Specifically, it seems, the more group expectations take account of idiosyncrasies of participants—so that personal predilections to behave actively or passively are integrated with role expectations—the less are partial records of interaction likely to provide valid measures of the members' relative centrality.

One more point has to do with the time-scale of observations compared with the time-scale of the group's duration. In most experimental groups, the two are virtually identical, the period of observation being about equal to the duration of the group's active existence. The same is obviously not true of most groups outside the confines of a laboratory. The point is almost self-evident, but needs nevertheless to be made, that the validity of the measured cen-

---

[3] See, for example, the account of a meeting of the *cuaird* in Arensberg and Kimball (1940, pp. 183-187). O'Donoghue, who is the leader and through whom "comments and questions are phrased" (p. 184) only on occasion says anything and "initiates nothing" (p. 183).

trality is highly influenced by the adequacy of the sample of inter-action sequences on which it is based. Short-run deviations can be expected to occur in most meetings of most groups, and estimates of centrality based on observations of a single meeting of a durable group are probably seldom valid.

Concerning the use of subjective estimates of interaction rates, there is little to add to what was said about observation. One should know the approximate frequency with which each member inter-acted with each of the others singly and collectively. For gauging centrality over short-run periods such estimates may be reasonably reliable and valid (Festinger and Hutte, 1954, p. 519; Bates and Cloyd, 1956, p. 32). But they probably become increasingly unre-liable as the period of time for which centrality is being calculated increases, owing to difficulties of recall and the greater salience of more recent events. In a study of discussion groups (described in Chapter 4 below), I asked group members at the end of the sixth week who usually talked "too much" and who usually talked "too little." Comparing the rank orders derived from their responses with each of the weekly rankings on participation which group lead-ers supplied, I found, as would be expected, that they correlated highly with the leaders' rankings for the fifth and sixth weeks, mod-erately with the leaders' rankings for the third and fourth weeks, and even more moderately with the leaders' rankings for the first and second weeks.

If the investigator asks only for gross participation rates, for ex-ample, by asking merely who participates most in discussions, valid-ity may be considerably reduced. Besides being subject to the limi-tations noted above on the use of partial observational records, answers to such questions may be greatly affected by the tendency of members to perceive actual participation in relation to expected par-ticipation. If members' estimates are affected by how much partic-ipation they had expected from each other, and in durable groups they probably always would be, the resulting data would sometimes understate the participation of the most active, and overstate the participation of the least active, and at other times the reverse bias would occur.

One more point about centrality might be made here. Homans comments on interaction that "our observations of this element can often be rather precise and definite, which gives them infinite charm for persons of a certain temperament" (1950, p. 37). Cen-trality is in this respect even more interesting than plain interac-tion: it is relatively easy to manipulate and its causal role can thus be experimentally verified. Two procedures have been used effectively, one being the Bavelas communications net and the other, instructions to the group discussion leaders to play active or passive roles.[4] In addition, the results of several studies suggest that one can plant deviants and affect centrality (e.g., Schachter, 1953, pp. 223-248), and there is some evidence that centrality can be manipulated by varying seating arrangements (Steinzor, 1955, pp. 348-353).

NORMATIVE CONSENSUS

The principal measurement problem affecting observability, consensus, and, to some extent, influence concerns the construction of the standard against which a member's observability, conformity, or influence is gauged, namely, the analyst's estimate of the contents of the group's normative consensus. Remarkably little systematic attention has been paid to this concept. Aside from the vague rules of procedure occasionally set down in an appendix by an anthropologist reporting a field study, few discussions of relevant measurement procedures exist.

Measurement ordinarily is of "group opinion," which is ascertained on a few limited topics in order to see whether the group in question has an opinion on these particular topics and, if so, which members agree with or conform to the group's opinions, or which members know accurately the state of group opinion on the topics. The methodological questions usually raised consequently bear on the relatively technical issues of weighting, subtraction, and the like: Should each member's views be counted equally in ascertaining the group's opinion, or should the leaders' views be given extra weight and the marginal members' views discounted? Should the member's own views be included when the purpose of ascertaining group opinion is to gauge his conformity and the group is small?

However, a group's opinions on specific topics do not constitute its normative consensus. As defined in Chapter 2, its normative consensus refers to the set of ideas and sentiments to which the members are motivationally and morally committed—each feels he and the others ought to hold, express, and act in accord with them—and in terms of which the members sanction one another, positively for compliance and negatively for deviance. From the

---

[4] See Bavelas (1951). On instructions to leaders, the earliest experiment I know of that utilizes this technique is reported in Lewin, Lippitt, and White (1939).

point of view of measurement there are several problems here.

One concerns the adequacy of the set of statements (each of which presumably reflects a possible "norm") as a sample of the full set of norms actually operative in guiding and regulating behavior in the group.[5] A second concerns the adequacy of any one statement as an indicator of an idea or sentiment that is normative in the group. Presumably, one would want to know several things from each member about each statement: How strongly does he feel about the matter? Does he think he is expected by other members to have a particular feeling, and how strong are such pressures? Does he think one or another feeling about the matter ought to be exhibited by the members or ought to be sanctioned if it is? And so forth. A third, related to the first, concerns the structure, organization, or hierarchy of a group's norms: their relative salience, felt consistency or inconsistency, weighted importance, and so forth. A fourth, of particular importance here, is the degree of consensus, in the sense of the extent to which the operative expectations, over all the activities in which members engage and over the range of their interactions, are norms that are commonly held or shared.

These remarks are intended to do no more than indicate the gross inadequacy of most measures of group opinion as indicators of normative consensus, and the consequent need for better ones. Some steps have been taken. For example, Bates and Cloyd (1956) describe an interesting procedure. They first write down as many presumably normative statements as they can which they consider pertinent to the group being studied and then ask each member to assume the role of informant and to estimate whether or not a majority shares the sentiment expressed by each statement and, if so, how important the sentiment is in the group. Using this technique to estimate the content of consensus may, though, interfere with its subsequent use in measuring the members' relative observability.

It is of interest to note that this same technique was suggested by Rousseau—whose analysis of the relation between the will of all and the general will remains one of the best discussions of the relation between the summarized responses of individuals and the collective property they are supposed to indicate:

[5] A similar point is made, though with reference to a slightly different problem, by Gross, et al. (1957, p. 113).

When in the popular assembly a law is proposed, what the people is asked is not exactly whether it approves or rejects the proposal, but whether it is in conformity with the general will, which is their will. Each man, in giving his vote, states his opinion on that point; and the general will is found by counting votes. When therefore the opinion that is contrary to my own prevails, this proves neither more nor less than that I was mistaken, and that what I thought to be the general will was not so (Rousseau, *The Social Contract*, Book IV, Chapter 2).

One of Rousseau's concerns was not so much that a "vote" might reflect an individual's particular interests—such votes he thought would presumably cancel each other out—but that it might reflect a person's membership in some subgroup, and not his membership in the political community. The voter might confuse the general will of the subgroup with the general will of the political community, since both stand above him, and might act in the political community in terms of a morality appropriate to a subgroup.

In making inferences from the responses of individuals to the sentiments of groups, this of course remains a potent source of error and suggests that more perhaps should be done to make respondents aware of their membership in the group under study. For example, questions might be so phrased that they placed the respondent squarely in his role as a member (e.g., How do you and the other members like you feel about x?), or define the group as the relevant reference group (What would other members think of your doing x?), or turn the respondent into a representative of his group to the interviewer (Speaking for the group, how would you people feel about x?); and so forth. Again, the situation in which questionnaires are filled out or interviews conducted could be used to make the respondent's membership more or less salient to him. For example, if a member were surrounded by other members when he answered questions intended to tap group-anchored opinions, he would probably respond in terms of his feelings as a member more often than he would if he were alone when answering them. Alternatively, in order to have respondents give opinions that are as "personal" as possible—which here means, that are independent of this membership group—one would want to instruct them to answer according to their own feelings on the matter, as distinct from the feelings of others, and privacy should characterize the situation in which the questionnaire or interview were administered.[6]

INFLUENCE

March (1955, 1956) reviews and compares several common methods of measuring "influence." The following remarks on some of the more or less standard kinds of measures bear only on their validity as indicators of influence as defined in this essay.

1. Measures derived from members' *pre-interaction* estimates of one another's influence. Data of this sort reflect members' views on how much influence each usually exercises, is likely to exercise, or is expected to exercise, and so pertain less to influence than to rank, though they do not provide very good indicators of that property either.

2. Measures derived from members' *post-interaction* estimates of one another's influence. For measuring members' relative influence during an immediately preceding period of interaction, estimates of the influence each exercised over "the group" would probably provide reasonably valid indicators. Assessments of this sort are often affected by situational and psychological factors, however, and for each case one would want to know something about the conditions under which the estimates were made, in order to be sure they were not systematically biased. For example, in groups having well-defined, differentiated, and clearly ranked roles, members see each other's performances in the light of the differential expectations. (An ingenious experiment by Sherif establishes this point for perceptions of performance where the results are ambiguous, Sherif, White, and Harvey [1955].) Subjective estimates of influence may therefore reflect differences in rank as well. When estimates of this sort refer to the influence members exercise not over "the group" but over the member who is answering the question, the respondent is encouraged to answer less in terms of rank but more in terms of his personal relations with each of the others. In general, such estimates of influence can be considered valid to the extent that the members rate each other much as a nonparticipant observer would.

3. Measures derived from a comparison of the opinions members express individually before interaction occurs and the decisions the

[6] See Banks (1957), who reports comparisons between the results of group interviews and individual interviews. The two methods give markedly different findings in several instances.

group reaches following a period of interaction. The logic of this kind of procedure seems to come as close to that called for by the concept of influence as any. What is lacking in these comparisons is the specifically action component, and they sometimes suffer from the Sherif effect. The decision, especially in an *ad hoc* group, is often a compromise between the extreme views represented in the group, with the result that the member who initially holds a middling position may be scored as influential, even if he makes not a single comment or gesture throughout the discussion. Consequently, such measures should be validated by information showing that the individuals' initial opinions were in fact those each expressed during the discussion.

For periods of time longer than a discussion session the same general idea can be used. One checks opinions held, expressed, and defended against various measures of consensus during the period of observation. It is necessary to keep in mind in this case that the concept specifies actions having effects on the state of consensus. The influential members are therefore those whose actions can be judged to affect consensus, not those whose opinions were merely "ahead of the group's opinions." Priority is less important than propagation, and origination probably less important than persistence.

4. Observers' ratings on "leadership" or "influence." The validity of these ratings depends, of course, on the criteria the observers use. If the criteria are framed relative to the concept or correspond to it, the resulting ratings probably provide reasonably valid measures.

5. Measures derived from interaction rates. In our terms, such rates indicate centrality, not influence.

In summary, having subjects estimate one another's influence is a possibility, though it is subject to the invalidity that affects most subjective estimates of objective conditions. Comparing the opinions of the members at different times, especially before and after group decisions, is probably the most valid procedure, and it is made even more valid if those who score high on influence are shown to have expressed, during the discussions, the opinions they held beforehand. If this procedure were used in conjunction with satisfactory measures of normative consensus, a highly valid set of measurements of influence would be obtained. Finally, ratings by observers may provide valid measures, depending on the criteria used to make the ratings.

[3]

Fifteen Propositions

No theory can be more sophisticated than the facts with which
it deals.

George C. Homans, *The Human Group*

Yet we cannot afford to become imprisoned in the framework of
fact that happens to be at hand, even if breaking out of this narrow framework means leaving demonstrated fact for acknowledged
conjecture.

Robert K. Merton, in Part One of Lazarsfeld
and Merton, *"Friendship as a Social Process"*

The five status-properties—rank, centrality, observability, conformity, and influence—taken two at a time, can be combined
to form twenty statements of simple implication. Fifteen of
these are of theoretic or empirical interest and are discussed in
this chapter. Each is considered more or less in its own right
and without regard for the others (aside from the basic logical
relations) in terms of its plausibility in the light of available
factual materials and its reasonableness in the light of generally
accepted theoretical ideas. Not until the next chapter are the
propositions seen as systematically interrelated and the set of
them considered as stating a theory of influence in small groups.

The fifteen assertions to be discussed are divided, for reasons
given shortly, into nine basic propositions or postulates and six
derivations. They are:

For any member of a small group:

I. 1. The higher his rank, the greater his centrality.
    2. The greater his centrality, the greater his observability.
    3. The higher his rank, the greater his observability (derivation).
    4. The greater his centrality, the greater his conformity.
 . 5. The higher his rank, the greater his conformity (derivation).

II. 6. The greater his observability, the greater his conformity.
     7. The greater his conformity, the greater his observability.
     8. The greater his observability, the greater his influence.
     9. The greater his conformity, the greater his influence.
    10. The greater his centrality, the greater his influence (derivation).
    11. The greater his influence, the greater his observability (derivation).
    12. The greater his influence, the greater his conformity.

III. 13. The higher his rank, the greater his influence (derivation).
     14. The greater his influence, the higher his rank.
     15. The greater his centrality, the higher his rank (derivation).

As stated above, the principal aim of the chapter is to show that these assertions are consistent with generally accepted ideas of a similar sort and with findings from a variety of studies. Nevertheless, it is worth while to point ahead at this time to the interpretation to be given the set of statements in the following chapters. It has perhaps been noticed that there are nine basic propositions, whereas the number logically required to generate the statements is less. This is because in the theory proper there are nine substantively important relations among the properties. Briefly, these are the following: rank is held to lead to centrality; centrality to observability and conformity; these two to one another and to influence; influence, in one direction, back to conformity and, in the other, back to rank; and so on, as in the figure below:

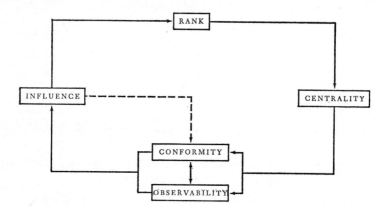

Six of the possible derivations from these basic propositions are discussed because of their theoretical or empirical interest, and the other five are not discussed because they are not particularly interesting.

Since the chapter is long and the analysis sometimes involved, the fifteen propositions have been divided, for purposes of presentation, into three groups. The first (I) contains relations among rank, centrality, observability, and conformity; the second (II), relations among centrality, conformity, observability, and influence; and the third (III), relations among rank, influence, and centrality.

Part I

1. For any member of a small group, the higher his rank, the greater his relative centrality.

This first proposition is a critical one, the general idea being that differences in rank among the members of a group function to order or to organize interaction sequences. Rank differences are probably most important in this way for the interaction that occurs in the course of set events and least important for the sequences occurring between pairs of members that are segregated from the others or for some other reason not directly visible to them. It is partly for this reason—that is, because the importance of rank in organizing interaction seems to vary directly with the proportion of the members present and participating—that attention is concentrated throughout on groups having the bulk of their activities in the form of set events.

The general idea in this proposition has been stated at one time or another by a number of theorists. Its use by Homans in *The Human Group* is, however, the principal stimulus for its use here and the immediate source of this particular version.

There appear to be several reasons for the relationship between rank and centrality—the greater weight which the higher-ranking members' actions have as sanctions and the consequent greater hesitancy of the lower-ranking members to speak up, the priority given (in speaking, etc.) to higher-ranking members or their assumption of it, the tendency for higher rank to be associated with greater "responsibility," perhaps certain fairly basic psychological states that come into play in social situations marked by rank differences, and so forth. More will be said about this fundamental proposition later.

With respect to relevant empirical materials, some studies presenting pertinent systematic data are the following:

:

Stephan and Mishler (1952) found that in Princeton tutorials, those in the higher-ranking status of instructor received, on the average, over half of the actions directed toward a particular member, while those in the lower-ranking status of student received, on the average, less than 10 percent of such actions. For the full set of 81 meetings observed, instructors figured as recipients or communicators in over 90 percent of the 11,000 participations recorded (which include participations "to the group").

Lippitt (1949, ch. 11) reports that a group of Michigan social scientists gave a training course in human relations skills to about 45 social workers and studied the operation and effectiveness of the workshop training sessions at the same time. There were three workshops ($N = 14, 16,$ and 17), each with a faculty "leader" who was not to lecture but to stimulate discussions among the participants. Even so, the centrality of the higher-ranking leaders is clearly evident from the reported data. Over some eighty-six hours of training (which was the total active life of each of the workshops), acts initiated averaged about 190 per hour for the three groups. Of these, one third (about 63 acts) were initiated by the leaders. The median member participation rate per hour was about 10 acts; the average range of member participation per hour was from about 1.5 acts to about 21 acts.

These two are both field studies. Experimental evidence is somewhat more difficult to come by, because so often experimenters either aim to minimize rank differences or simply ignore them. The following are two ingenious experiments using quite different techniques for creating controlled rank differences.

From professionals concerned with mental health problems in a medium-sized city, Hurwitz and his colleagues (1953) chose 24 who were rated by people familiar with the personnel in the field as having high professional rank and 24 who were rated

as having (relatively) low professional rank. These 48 subjects
were invited to attend an all-day conference on mental health;
42 came. At this "conference," they were divided into a total
of 32 different groups, each of which had 5 or 6 participants
and 8 of which met simultaneously. Each subject thus participated in 4 different groups over the course of the day, and in
none was he with any of the people he had been with in
another. The initial ratings were validated by "perceived power"
subjective ratings at the beginning of the conference. Over all
32 groups, the higher-ranking participants both initiated and received more communications than the lower-ranking participants.

An equally imaginative experiment, in which role-playing is
used to good effect, is reported by Zander and Cohen (1955).
Students were formed into committees of five, in which they
were to discuss as realistically as possible what they should do
with an anonymous bequest to the university. Two other students joined the committee, one as a "dean" and the other as a
"freshman"; the other committee members were informed of
the new members' statuses but the incumbents were not, and
they therefore participated unaware of the statuses others ascribed to them. The "dean" interacted more frequently than
the "freshman" in all committees observed.

Bales (1952, p. 153) reports something similar for his discussion
groups—"Groups with no designated leader generally tend to
have more equal participation than groups with designated
leaders of higher status"—but no details are given.

The hypothesis, then, is reasonably well confirmed. A summary way of phrasing the results of these studies is to say that
the frequency with which any one member interacts with another depends upon the latter's relative rank: The higher the
other's rank, relative to the ranks of all members, the more a
member interacts with him instead of with others.

It should be noted, however, that if rank is an important

determinant of the patterning of who-to-whom exchanges in a group, so, too, are several other factors, such as possession of important information, physical location, friendship, "popularity," and so forth. These are all "external factors," as far as the present conceptualization of an interaction system is concerned, but under certain circumstances they may well play such an important part that rank and centrality become dissociated. In the next chapter, some effects which external factors may have on centrality are discussed as potential disturbances of the system. (Also, see below, in this chapter, the discussion of Proposition 13.)

2. For any member of a small group, the greater his centrality relative to other members, the greater his observability.

As was mentioned when centrality was discussed, many have noticed a connection between things roughly corresponding to what is meant here by centrality and observability. Besides the explicit and implicit statements concerning the connection in the works cited above, assertions of the following sort occur on occasion.

In presenting some general ideas on the practical effectiveness of the group-decision technique in changing opinions, Kurt Lewin writes:

> Of course, there is a great difference in asking for a decision after a lecture or after a discussion. . . . A group discussion gives the leader a better indication of where the audience stands and what particular obstacles have to be overcome (1952, p. 465).

Festinger and his colleagues, listing reasons why a member of a housing unit or court is not affected by "group standards," state:

> There may not be sufficient communication between the member and others in the group. Under these conditions the

pressures from the group are simply not brought to bear on the member although, if they had been exerted, they might have been very effective. In such instances the deviate *may not even be aware* of the fact that he is different from most of the others in his group (1953, p. 217; emphasis added).

In an experiment using communication nets, Heise and Miller found that a net in which one position is the link between the other two proved superior in efficiency to one in which anyone can talk to anyone else. The first is more efficient, they reason,

> . . . because the reconstruction of sentences [which was the task] requires more integration of group activity; the central man can coordinate and place in the proper context the words that the Ss contribute. He is in a position *to detect and correct* mistaken words and incorrect hypotheses. Conversely, the situation can become chaotic in net 1, for no one organizes the individual contributions (1955, p. 362; emphasis added).

Such statements, of course, are hardly evidence supporting the hypothesis. Like the proposition itself, they are justifiable on the grounds that interaction is "communicative," it conveys information, and one who interacts frequently in a group is thus more likely than one who does not to be aware of the ways of that group. Yet, despite the apparent agreement on this general idea and on its derivatives, no study has yet been reported, as far as I know, which includes among its principal aims the testing of this hypothesis. And in only one of a number of research reports examined is there any systematic data at all relevant to the assertion's plausibility.

R. M. W. Travers (1941, pp. 50-51) had the students of a large Teachers' College class, which discussed contemporary issues each week, estimate the class's opinions on 25 "issues of the day." Participation in the weekly discussion, as judged by observers (who used some unspecified criteria), is reported to be positively related to accuracy of estimates but not to a statistically significant extent.

In order to present some material bearing on the hypothesis, I report here a very simple study I carried out on a single evening class for adults some time ago. Observability (knowledge of consensus) I attempted to measure by having each student ($N = 27$) indicate for each of six normative statements on student-instructor relations (e.g., "Instructors should spend about half of each class reviewing reading assignments") (a) whether he agreed or disagreed with the statement and (b) whether he thought the majority of the class would agree with it. To measure centrality I asked each student to estimate the number of others in the class whom he (1) knew by name, (2) would join at a table in the cafeteria, (3) had ever spoken to, and (4) would stop to speak with outside of class. On each of these the median of the distribution was used as the cutting point, students thus being classified as "high" or "low" on centrality by four different criteria. A student "correctly" estimated group opinion if he had said, for a statement that more than half of the class had in fact endorsed, that the majority would agree with it. (The majority agreed with three of the six statements and disagreed with the other three.) Altogether, then, there were 24 comparisons available for "testing" the hypothesis that centrality and knowledge of consensus are associated. Nineteen of the 24 were in the "predicted" direction. The first two centrality indicators (knowing the others' names and joining them in the cafeteria) are of questionable relevance, and if they are not used, 11 of the remaining 12 comparisons were favorable to the hypothesis.

In summary, however, evidence relating to this hypothesis is almost totally lacking, despite the fairly widespread acceptance of the general principle from which it derives.

3. For any member of a small group, the higher his rank, the greater his observability.

This third proposition derives from the preceding two and its rationale is essentially that of its premises. In addition, statements very much like it but predicated of personnel in complex organizations are beginning to take their place in the theory of authority. Merton, for example, writes at some length about the requirement "that those in authority have substantial knowledge of [group] norms; a greater knowledge, presumably, than that held by other individual members of the group" (1957, pp. 336-353). And here as elsewhere in this essay, Homans' analysis in *The Human Group* (1950) is highly relevant.

The major piece of evidence for the assertion is a study done a number of years ago by Chowdhry and Newcomb (1955) on the ability of leaders and members to estimate group opinion.

The sample consisted of the members of four groups, ranging in size from 23 to 40 (so that whether they conform to the definition of a small group is questionable). For each group three degrees of rank were identified by means of four nomination questions: Which three persons (a) are most capable of acting as president, (b) influence group opinion most, (c) are most worthy of acting as representatives, and (d) would you most like to be friends with? Members were scored by the total number of times they were nominated. The "leaders" in each group were the 20 percent who received the largest number of votes; the "members" were those who received some votes but not as many; and the "isolates" were those who were not mentioned at all. For the four groups:

Rank	Religious Group	Political Group	Medical Fraternity	Medical Sorority
Leader	23	22	20	20
Member	46	48	60	65
Isolate	31	30	20	15
	100%	100%	100%	100%
Base	26	23	30	40

Observability was measured by estimates of group opinion on matters having three degrees of presumed relevance to the group or of familiarity to the members. Every item was scored twice by a respondent, once to indicate his opinion and once to indicate his estimate of the percentage of the group that would endorse it. Error scores for each member were computed (1) by subtracting his estimates from the corresponding actual proportions who agreed with the items and then (2) by averaging his divergences.

On the items of high relevance in each group, the mean error score of the leaders was lower than the mean error score of the members and of isolates, over all four groups without exception, 5 of the 8 comparisons being statistically significant.

In contrast to this result are findings from two or three other studies sometimes cited as if they contradicted the outcome of the Chowdhry-Newcomb research.

One such study, by Talland (1954), reportedly followed the previous one in design but did not confirm the findings. A careful reading of Talland's description of his methods, however, yields no sign of his having measured observability at all. Rather, in our terms, he measured conformity. The "accuracy of evaluating group opinion was measured by the rank correlation coefficient between each member's individual rank scale and the ranked summated scale" (*ibid.*, p. 432). That is, Talland asked members of psychotherapy groups to order fifteen topics "with a view to their usefulness to the group" and then compared each member's ordering with a composite ordering secured by combining the individuals' orderings. His findings, in consequence, are of no relevance in the present context.

A second allegedly pertinent research is the Hites-Campbell study (1950) of eight Ohio State University fraternities. The members of each gave their responses to a 19-item questionnaire and estimated the fraternity's responses. Leaders were of two types, those in office by election and those in office by appointment. The results appear to show that leaders are no more able than ordinary members to estimate group opinion correctly. However, the "opinions" or "attitudes" measured in this study are not easily shown to be "group" opinions or attitudes: of the five areas of opinion studied, two seem patently to include neither norms nor values nor status definitions, so that only three areas remain—opinions about leadership, about other members, and about the physical environment. Since there are eight fraternities, 24 comparisons are available, and elected leaders (for appointed leaders are not necessarily high-ranking) have lower error scores than nonleaders in 15 of them. Of the 9 reversals, 5 are contributed by two fraternities; this appears to be for substantive reasons (indicated by "lower" consensus), but nevertheless, if we exclude them here without going into the reasons why this is legitimate, elected leaders are more accurate than nonleaders in 14 of the remaining 18 comparisons. Hites and Campbell's findings are, then, not unambiguously negative in character. Nevertheless, because the "attitudes" they measured are too conglomerate to provide adequate tests of the hypothesis, and because, with so few items per opinion area, the "attitudes" are probably unreliably measured, their results cannot be used as either favorable or unfavorable evidence for Proposition 3.

A study by Gage and Exline (1953) also attempted to relate opinion estimate scores to "leadership" but found no correlation. In this case, however, there seems to have been some mix-up in the measurement of "accuracy," for the participants first completed a 100-item questionnaire, then spent a fair amount of time in discussions, and then both estimated group opinion on 50 of the items and nominated members as leaders. Insofar as the discussions had any effect on opinions—which presumably they did, since the topic being discussed was the one the items concerned—the "group opinion" which was measured and in terms of which accuracy was gauged was not the same opinion the members were estimating.

In short, then, this hypothesis is not at all well tested, only one of the studies ostensibly dealing with it being methodologically sound. Its findings are what one would expect if rank and observability were associated, but none of the others, except perhaps part of the Hites-Campbell study, can be considered relevant.

4. For any member of a small group, the greater his centrality, the greater his conformity.

The principal theoretical basis for this proposition is that interaction has more or less subtle socializing effects, so that, in general, the more a member interacts with others of his group, the more socialized or conforming he becomes. I do not think the point needs further comment.

However, it is unlikely that the proposition can be exemplified by data from the kinds of studies being reviewed at this point. For the idea here is that over fairly long periods of time, centrality and conformity come to be associated. But we do not usually have measurements taken over long periods of time, nor do we have conformity measured extensively. What can be shown is that centrality and conformity, in the limited sense of acceptance of a group decision or group judgment, tend to be correlated, but, as mentioned in the last chapter, acceptance measures are of unknown validity as indicators of conformity in the broader sense. The negative version of the proposition, namely, that the less central a member is, the less he conforms, is the more easily exemplified and is the version used in the following summaries. (Strictly speaking, this version is the negation of a proposition not otherwise discussed, that conformity implies centrality.)

Centrality, it was noted earlier, may be experimentally controlled through instructions to "leaders," some being instructed to play an active part and others a passive part. Some leaders are to enter fully into the discussion in their respective groups and to give their own ideas on the matters being talked about (active leadership), and other leaders are to refrain from discussing content altogether in their respective groups and to take part, if at all, only in order to guide the discussion (passive leadership).[1] Usually in studies of this sort the findings are presented as comparisons between the two types of leaders and are thus comparisons between positions in two different groups. Since our interest is in the comparison between positions within a group or type of group, it is necessary to compromise and to have the hypothesis read, the less central a leader is in a group, the less likely he is to accept a group decision.

Hare (1955, p. 558) studied these two leadership roles by running discussions on camping equipment among groups of Boy Scouts. The group decision consisted of a ranking of various pieces of equipment in terms of their importance for survival. The more peripheral, passive leaders (Hare's "supervisory" leaders) should, if the hypothesis is to be confirmed, show less acceptance of group decisions than the more central, active leaders (his "participatory" leaders). Acceptance (conformity) is measured by the correlation between the ranking of the pieces which the group arrived at publicly at the close of the discussion and its leader's and followers' post-session individual rankings. The differences are minuscule but in the right direction. (The rank-order correlation coefficients reported below, and in subsequent tables of a similar sort, are of course averages of the individual coefficients within each class of participant):

Kind of Group	(A) Leaders	(B) Followers	(A − B) Difference
Actively led	.98	.96	.02
Passively led	.80	.86	−.06

[1] Evidence concerning the difference in centrality between these leadership roles is given in Stephan and Mischler (1952, p. 606).

Preston and Heintz (1953, p. 576) obtained comparable results using approximately the same procedures. In their study, the population was composed of college students and the discussion concerned 12 possible candidates for the U. S. Presidency. Again, conformity is measured by correlating each person's post-session ranking of the men with his group's ranking and obtaining the average coefficient for the leaders and followers separately in each kind of group.

Kind of Group	(A) Leaders	(B) Followers	(A − B) Difference
Actively led	.72	.86	−.14
Passively led	.31	.75	−.44

Somewhat the same result is reported by Maier and Solem (1953). In this case the active and passive leadership styles are used by people called, respectively, "leaders" and "observers." The discussion concerned the horse-trading problem (which has a correct answer). The participants' answers were scored before and after the discussion but a group decision was reached only in some cases. Properly speaking, acceptance is not at issue here but only the effects of discussion. Those who are most active in the discussion, though, should—if the reasoning behind the proposition linking centrality and conformity is correct— be those who are most affected by it. Among those who began with the wrong answer, then, the more active participants should more often change to the correct one. (Most groups changed toward the correct answer.) Over the set of 67 groups, 194 of the 353 participants began with the wrong answer. Of these, 115 changed to the right answer. The proportions within each of the three classes of participants, ordered according to their presumed rates of participation, are as follows (p. 568):

Leaders	79%	(15/19)
Members	60%	(96/161)
Observers	21%	(4/14)

The hypothesis, then, is plausible in the light of some available evidence. It should be pointed out, though, that these findings are consistent with an interpretation that views the centrality-conformity relationship not as a direct connection between them, owing to the continuing pressures under which the more central members are placed in virtue of their centrality, but as an indirect relationship, owing to the influence which the central members exercise and in virtue of which their opinions, judgments, etc. are more congruent with group opinion or group judgment than the opinions or judgments of those who do not exercise much influence. Considerable attention is paid to this matter in Part II of the chapter.

5. For any member of a small group, the higher his rank, the greater his conformity.

Proposition 5 derives from Propositions 1 and 4, relating rank to centrality and centrality to conformity, and the principal argument in its support is contained in its premises: that is, higher-ranking members, because they are more central and hence more subject to socialization and social control processes than others, should also conform more to group norms. It contains both Theorems 3 and 5 in the paper, "Compliant Actions," by Zetterberg (1957, pp. 190, 193), who cites in support of the theorems results from Newcomb's Bennington study and from an experiment by Back.

It might appear that use has been made here of yet another theme running through Homans' treatise (1950), since a relation between rank and "conformity" is repeatedly stated there. It is evident, however, that Homans often uses the term *conformity* to refer to what is here called compliance—for example, "The higher the rank of a person within a group, the more nearly his activities conform to the norms of the group" (p. 141)—and hence is referring to the relationship discussed below under the heading of rank and influence.

Merei (1952), though, does discuss this relation between rank and normative conformity, emphasizing in particular, it would seem, an inference from it, that insofar as the members perceive the relationship, what higher-ranking members do or say is likely to be taken as indicating what the norms are; that is, the relationship, if publicly recognized, enters into the relationship between rank and influence. The point is important and is discussed more fully later.

Among the researches providing evidence in support of the assertion is one by Torrance (1955), who studied combat crews containing three men (pilot, navigator, and gunner).

Crews discussed four topics, the horse-trading problem, the number of dots on a card, the "stories" they wrote about a conference scene, and how they would act if downed in enemy territory. Conformity is here measured by "acceptance" data and so is limited to the members' relative conformity on single items. Rank is indicated by the rank of the member's differentiated functional role, the pilot having the highest rank *within the crew* and the gunner the lowest. (The emphasis is needed because the navigator may be a higher-ranking officer than the pilot.) On the second and fourth topics data are reported that can be used here. On the Dot Test each man gave his own estimate, the estimates were discussed, a crew decision was reached, and then each again gave his own estimate. The mean deviancy scores (difference between crew estimates and individuals' final estimates) ranged from about 450 to 700 for pilots, 825 to 900 for navigators, and 950 to 1150 for gunners. Pilots, apparently, were less "resistant" to or more "accepting" of the crew's estimates than were gunners or navigators. In the survival problem, 77 percent of the pilots said they were in complete agreement with the crew decision reached, compared with 60 percent of the navigators and 53 percent of the gunners.

The acceptance by the pilots of the crews' decisions may be, at least in part, more apparent than real: Their conformity with the decision may result not so much from their having been influenced more than the navigators or gunners as from their having exercised more influence than the others.

In either case, centrality appears to be the important intervening condition, critical to both the rank-conformity and the rank-influence relationships, and its role in relation to conformity and influence is examined in detail in the second part of this chapter, to which we now turn.

Part II

6. For any member of a small group, the greater his observability, the greater his conformity.

There is probably a fairly strong direct relationship between observability and conformity, with variations in the extent to which a member is aware of group norms being accompanied by parallel variations in the extent to which he is committed to the norms. Both the "social reality" thesis (e.g., Festinger, 1953, pp. 4-5) and reference group theory (e.g., Merton, 1957, pp. 225-386), for example, assume some such relationship, not to mention its use in various socialization theories.

It is, nevertheless, a qualified relationship, and one for which apparently supporting evidence is particularly liable to result from the presence of a third factor that is strongly related to both. Conformity certainly does not invariably depend upon observability, since (as Proposition 4 above states) fairly subtle reinforcing and socializing effects can occur without a member's being particularly aware of the normative commitments that are being maintained or developed. Nor does awareness of norms invariably increase one's commitment to them. Finally, even if the two properties do in fact vary together as expected, this may be because of their separate relationships to centrality (Propositions 2 and 4—which, however, do not logically entail Proposition 6).

For our limited purposes, data as pertinent as any come from suggestibility experiments in which "group norms" are announced. In none of these studies, however, at least as far as I know, are norms proper used. Instead, what participants conform to, or "accept," is some sort of group judgment, cognition, or decision. Goldberg's study (1954) of the effects on individuals' judgments of repeated exposure to a "group" judgment illustrates the procedure and type of finding.

Subjects first estimated the IQ's of people from photographs, then were exposed to the "group norm," and subsequently estimated the IQ's from the photographs again. The experimenter created the "exposure" and the "group norm" alike, for he announced the group score to each subject individually and the score he announced always differed by some specific amount from the particular subject's initial estimate. The "exposures," or announcements, are the experimental equivalents of observability, so that the relevant comparison is between the ever-exposed and the unexposed, who formed the controls. The subjects' estimates following exposure (observability) indicate their acceptance of the "group norm" (conformity). The result, which held over a number of variations, was that those exposed to the group norm modified their judgments in the direction of the announced norm, whereas those who were unexposed, the control subjects, did not modify their initial judgments very much one way or the other.[2]

[2] The experiment involved three degrees of exposure besides the control of no exposure, but no significant further modifications were induced by the larger number of exposures—which, under the circumstances and in the light of the present hypothesis, is reasonable, although the result ran counter to Goldberg's hypothesis. One other result is of interest: The further the "group" norm was made from the subjects' initial estimates, the greater the modification in their subsequent estimates. But although the modification in absolute numbers was greater, it was proportionately constant over three degrees of distance, the proportion being about 30 percent.
    Perhaps the most famous of these experiments are Asch's (1951, 1952, ch. 16) and Sherif's (1936, ch. 6; Sherif and Sherif, 1956, ch. 8).

In view of the number of such studies, the hypothesis must be considered as reasonably well supported.

7. *For any member of a small group, the greater his conformity, the greater his observability.*

The link that runs from conformity to observability is somewhat more complicated. There are probably certain psychological processes relevant to the relationship in this direction. For example, projection, the tendency to perceive social situations in terms of one's own sentiments and ideas, makes it likely that the more conforming members would also be those with the measurably more "accurate" perceptions of group norms. But of more importance here is the role of the sanctioning process.

As it usually operates, sanctioning provides varying degrees of information about group norms, depending upon the degree of conformity of the member receiving the sanctions. In the ordinary course of interaction, the responses from others signal whether and to what extent a member's line of action is in accord with their expectations. Positive sanctions support his line of action, and thereby indicate to him that his sentiments and ideas probably correspond to what is normative. Since he is likely to be aware of his own sentiments and ideas, such sanctions have the effect of indicating to him the content of the normative sentiments and ideas. Negative sanctions, on the other hand, at least the more common milder ones, indicate to the recipient only that his line of action is not appropriate and by implication that his corresponding sentiments and ideas probably diverge from what is normative. Unlike positive sanctions, they do not at the same time indicate to him what *is* normative.

Precisely because of his normative conformity, it is the more conforming member who, compared with his less conforming colleague, tends to behave in accord with others' expectations and hence to receive more positive sanctions and less negative sanctions than the latter. His greater conformity, in conjunction with the normal operation of the sanctioning process, thus affords him greater observability of the group's norms. (Two ideas used in this argument are stated below, in Propositions 9 and 14, which link conformity to influence via compliance, and influence to rank.)

There is a third concept related to conformity and observability which bears on this interpretation of the relationship between them. As it happens, an indicator of it is logically related to the usual indicators of observability and conformity, and it may be approached through this methodological relationship. At the descriptive level, as the following diagram shows, a common indicator of conformity (the similarity between a member's own opinions and actual group opinion) and a common indicator of observability (the similarity between his estimate of group opinion and actual group opinion) imply a third measure, which may be called "felt similarity" (the similarity between his own opinions and those he estimates to be group opinions) :[3]

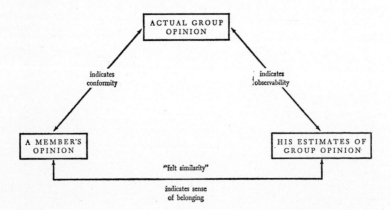

The relationships here—among an indicator of conformity, an indicator of observability, and "felt similarity"—are logical: the three are necessarily related. Considered by itself, though, the

[3] A similar formulation, including diagram, but with a slightly different interpretation, occurs in Gage and Exline (1953).

degree of similarity between the opinions a member attributes to himself and those he attributes to the group would also seem to be an indicator of a fairly basic concept, namely, the property of "alienation," or "sense of belonging," or "degree of identification with the group." If, for example, two members of a group who are known to differ in their degree of felt belonging first state their own opinions and then estimate group opinions, it would be reasonable to expect the one who feels he really belongs to attribute the same opinions to himself as he attributes to the group much more frequently than the one who does not feel he really belongs.

The methodological relation labeled "felt similarity" can thus be taken as indicating a member's sense of belonging. The latter is usually assumed to vary with the sanctions a member receives, being increased by positive sanctions and decreased by indifference and negative sanctions. The more conforming a member is, then, the more he should feel he is a part of the group and, at the descriptive level, the higher his "felt similarity" score should be. In short, the set of methodological relationships at the descriptive level seems to parallel the set of substantive relationships which the interpretation of the conformity-observability hypothesis above invoked.[4]

In any case, "felt similarity" is of use here independently of what it may indicate. For owing to its logical connections with certain indicators of observability and conformity, it can be used in place of one of these indicators. For example, if a member of a group (a) attributes similar opinions to himself and the group (felt similarity) and (b) holds opinions that in fact correspond to those of the group as a whole (which indicates conformity), then his estimate of group opinion necessarily is fairly accurate (which indicates observability). In some studies only correlations between felt similarity and measures of either conformity or observability are reported, and owing to these logical connec-

---

[4] Obviously, if one wants to study the relationships among conformity, sense of belonging, and observability, an indicator of sense of belonging other than "felt similarity" would have to be used.

tions, such correlations can be used to suggest the plausibility of Proposition 7.

Several studies bearing on this hypothesis are summarized below. In each of them it has been necessary to use felt similarity as indicating either conformity or observability. Also, in each only correlations are reported, and I have assumed that conformity was prior to and facilitated observability.

Wallen (1943) had the students of a small college each give his own opinion on three items and estimate the proportion of the college that would agree with each. In this case, felt similarity was strongly marked, and so those whose opinions were in the majority camp were much more likely than those whose opinions were not to have correctly estimated college opinion.

In the study referred to earlier, Travers (1941) reports similar results for his class on current affairs, namely, that because of the high degree of felt similarity, those whose own opinions in fact conformed to the majority opinion were the more accurate in their estimates of the class's opinions.

A study by Gage and Exline (1953) of four moderately durable discussion groups (with 15 to 22 members apiece) measured both the members' own opinions on the character, purpose, and importance of discussion groups and their estimates of their respective groups' opinions. At two different times and in each of the groups, the correlation between the members' felt similarity scores and their accuracy scores (observability) was high and positive and, consequently, the unreported correlation between conformity and accuracy (observability) was also high.

Similar results on a single attitude are reported by Gorden (1953).

8. *For any member of a small group, the greater his observability, the greater his influence.*
9. *For any member of a small group, the greater his conformity, the greater his influence.*

No systematic data pertaining to either of these hypotheses seem to exist yet. Presumably, a member is more likely to influence the group's normative consensus the more accurate his knowledge of it is; and, presumably, the more conforming he is, the more his behavior is likely to be in accord with group norms and thus to influence consensus by reinforcing the norms.

A passage in Merei (1952) reports observations that seem consistent with the observability-influence hypothesis, although it requires interpretation. Specifically, I interpret the "bent to remember" as referring to a knowledge of consensus and do not assume with Merei that this knowledge necessarily reflects a distinctly personal quality of individual leaders:

> During our investigations we observed that in some cases the leader brings a presocial group to a higher degree of concerted action, in other cases to a lower one. . . . Such raising or lowering of group level depends mostly on the personal qualities of the leader, especially on his capacity to organize. The capacity consists of *the bent to remember every custom,* to see to it that objects are returned where they belong and that the rituals are observed, even if these were learned from the group. The leader who has this quality raises the group level even if he totally submits to the group's traditions (1952, p. 327; emphasis added).

With respect to the conformity-influence hypothesis, another observation of Merei's is pertinent:

> . . . the curious situation obtains where the order-giver imitates, while the models follow the orders of their imitator (1952, p. 323).

A similar point apparently is made by Lippitt and his colleagues:

The behavior of a member in a high power position is sometimes perceived as representing group standards, and so his acts are spontaneously imitated as group-approved or group-desired acts (1953, p. 481).

The reasoning in this passage also suggests why conformity may be connected with other kinds of influence, such as the revision or extension of consensus, as well as with its reinforcement.

The relationships here, however, become somewhat complicated and can be more easily disentangled after the effects of influence on conformity and observability have been discussed (Propositions 11 and 12).

10. For any member of a small group, the greater his centrality, the greater his influence.

Proposition 10 derives logically from 2 and 8, or from 4 and 9, and its rationale lies in its premises: The more central members of a group should also be the more influential members, because centrality facilitates conformity and observability and they in turn facilitate influence.

Among the studies providing support for this hypothesis, and by inference for its premises, are the following:

In leaderless discussion groups, Bass (1949) reports, the correlation between talking time (centrality) and observers' ratings on "leadership" (influence) is .93.

Studying the family as a three-person group, Strodtbeck (1954) measured influence by his "revealed difference" technique and centrality by acts initiated, as scored with the Bales scheme. Each of 48 mother-father-son trios discussed nine issues; since Strodtbeck awarded 2 points per decision, a total of 864 points was scored. Of these, 44 percent were won by those who participated most in that particular discussion (the particular people of course participated more in some discussions than in others),

30 percent by those who were in the middle, and 26 percent by those who participated least.[5]

In the experiments run by March (1956, p. 263), to determine the consistency of various measures of "influence," the average rank-order correlations between total participation rates (centrality) and influence, as measured by a comparison of individuals' pre-interaction opinions with the group's post-interaction opinions, were positive but slight (.23 and .31). The correlations with subjective estimates of influence, both on the group and on the individual answering the question, were higher ($r = .58$ and .52, respectively).

These three studies provide some data in support of the assertion that a member's centrality and influence tend to be associated. The proposition states, though, that the two properties stand in a directional relationship, that centrality is a condition of influence. Evidence bearing on this point is given in studies where the researcher exercises some control over the centrality of at least some participants, as in studies where instructions are given to "leaders" to play a relatively active or a relatively passive role in discussions. As noted earlier, the comparisons in these studies are between positions in different groups (leaders in actively led groups vs. leaders in passively led groups), rather than between positions within groups (leaders vs. followers). By design, the active leader is more central in his group than the passive leader is in his, but it is not possible to

[5] The percentages are calculated from data presented in Table 3, p. 26. In the revealed-difference technique, the investigator determines from questionnaires completed by the respondents the matters on which there are two-against-one disagreements. He then reveals the existence of the disagreements to the members; in this case Strodtbeck revealed nine disagreements in three of which any one member found himself disagreeing with the other two. The participants then discuss the disagreement and the influence score is based upon how well the minority member is able to hold his own: if he persuades the others, he receives two points; if he holds his own, he receives one point and the others each get one half point; if he yields, they get one point apiece.

tell from the reports of these studies whether one, both, or neither kind of leader is more or less central than his respective followers. The hypothesis becomes, therefore: The greater the relative activity of one "leader" in one group, compared with the relative activity of a second "leader" in a second group, the greater the relative influence of the first leader compared with the relative influence of the second leader.

Hare's study (1955) of Boy Scouts and the Preston-Heintz study (1953) of college students, both referred to earlier, contain relevant data. Influence in both cases is measured by correlating a participant's pre-interaction ranking of whatever was discussed (pieces of camping equipment in one case, and possible nominees for the Presidency in the other) with the post-interaction ranking arrived at by the group. As is evident, neither kind of "leader" in the Preston-Heintz study was very influential, both being less influential than their respective "followers," but the difference between them on influence parallels, and presumably results from, the created difference between them on centrality. (As before, the rank-order correlation coefficients in the table are averages of the coefficients for each of the participants within each category and kind of group.)

Kind of Group	(A) Leaders	(B) Followers	(A − B) Difference
Hare's study			
Actively led	.77	.56	+ .21
Passively led	.50	.55	− .05
Preston-Heintz study			
Actively led	.25	.42	− .17
Passively led	.22	.52	− .30

This tenth hypothesis, then, seems to be reasonably well substantiated by available data.

11. *For any member of a small group, the greater his influence, the greater his observability.*

Proposition 11 is discussed below, along with Proposition 12, and so I will only say here that there is no good evidence for or against it. Talland (1954) asserts such a relationship between influence and observability on the basis of his findings, but, as was mentioned before, he does not appear to have measured observability (see the discussion above under Proposition 3).

12. *For any member of a small group, the greater his influence, the greater his conformity.*

The basic point here is that in virtue of exercising influence, and thus moving consensus toward the sentiments or ideas he holds, a member becomes more conforming than he was and in due course more conforming than others are. The explication of the hypothesis is more complicated than it may at first seem, however.

To begin, let us examine some seemingly pertinent findings:

Comparing once again the two kinds of leaders in the Hare (1955) and Preston-Heintz (1953) studies, we can see that the kind of leader who exercised more influence relative to his followers (the active leader) was also the more conforming relative to his followers. Influence is indicated as it was just above, and conformity is indicated as it was earlier, by the correlation between a participant's final ranking (of equipment or nominees) and his group's ranking. The full data for both having been given before (under Propositions 10 and 4, respectively), the table below (page 78) merely presents the "difference" figures. Hare's active "leaders" were both more influential and very slightly more conforming than their "followers," whereas his passive "leaders" were both slightly less influential and slightly less conforming than their "followers": *The difference between the two kinds of "leaders,"* which is what concerns us in all these comparisons, is thus as expected. In the Preston-Heintz study, neither the active nor the passive "leaders" were as influential or as conforming as their respective "followers"; however, the passive "leaders" were more *uninfluential* and more *nonconforming*, relative to their "followers," than the active "leaders" were relative to their "followers," and so, again, *the difference between the two kinds of leaders is as expected.*

Kind of Group	Influence (A − B) Difference	Conformity (A − B) Difference
Hare's study		
Actively led	.21	.02
Passively led	−.05	−.06
Preston-Heintz study		
Actively led	−.17	−.14
Passively led	−.30	−.44

As the sources of these figures suggest (i.e., Propositions 4 and 10), the association between influence and conformity may be owing to their common dependence on centrality. For the moment, though, let us interpret the association as resulting from the exercise of influence: The active leaders "accepted" the group decision to a greater extent, or were more conforming, than the passive leaders *because* they influenced the decision more in their groups than the passive leaders did in theirs. It is not that the active leaders were moved toward the group position (as a result of their centrality) but that they moved the group toward their own position (as a result of their influence).

It is necessary to proceed carefully here, however. Such a process probably does occur and it may have occurred in these groups, but the results as they stand are far from unambiguous. This is not only because they consist at best of showing that active leaders were both somewhat more influential than passive leaders and somewhat more conforming, or because each of these could have resulted from a common third factor. It is also because even these modest results may have arisen from the way "group opinion" is treated in these studies—as not forming until a collective judgment is publicly expressed—in conjunction with the particular measurement model the studies employ. In this model, the relation between a member's own opinion at Time 1 and group opinion at Time 2 (r_{12}) is considered indicative of the member's influence on group opinion; the relation between group opinion at Time 2 and the member's own opinion at Time 3 (r_{23}) is considered indicative of his conformity; there remains the relationship between the member's own opinions at Times 1 and 3 (r_{13}), which is considered indicative of the stability of his opinion or, inversely, of its instability and hence of the group's impact on his opinion—that is, of the extent to which he was influenced by the discussion. Diagrammatically:

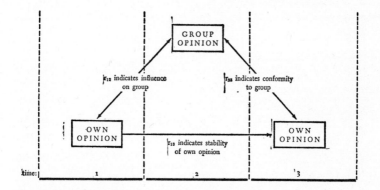

In this kind of measurement model, then, if influence *as measured* (r_{12}) is low and conformity as measured (r_{23}) is high, the measured impact of the group on the person's opinion *must* also be high(r_{13} is low, indicating instability). Alternatively, if influence as measured (r_{12}) is high and conformity as measured (r_{23}) is also high, the measured impact of the group *must* be low (r_{13} is high, indicating stability).

It does not take much imagination, though, to think of a situation where (1) a member's influence on group opinion is in fact low, and (2) the impact of the group on his own opinion is also low, but (3) his subsequent conformity with group opinion is high. Presumably these are the cases where his *initial* conformity with group opinion (which is not measured in these studies) is also high and where he does not in fact take much part in the discussions prior to the group decision. Such conforming non-participators would in this measurement model be judged as influentials. It should also be possible, but is not in this model, for a member to have influenced the group considerably, and to be highly conforming subsequently, but also to have changed his own opinion radically in the course of the discussions. There are, then, grounds for doubting the validity of the method used to measure influence. (The measurement of conformity seems *prima facie* more valid, although the conception of "group opinion" is restrictively narrow.)

Nevertheless, the substantive point the data suggest is important, even if they are not quite adequate to establish it, and I shall proceed on the assumption that the exercise of influence may on occasion lead to conformity for the reason given, namely, that through influencing group opinion, one moves it closer to his own position and thereby becomes more conforming than others are or than he himself was.

In the active-passive leadership studies, to return now to them, the active leaders were not only the more influential and the more conforming; they were also, by design, the more central. The question raised before recurs: Are centrality and conformity associated mainly because the more central members are more influenced by the group (Proposition 4)? Or are the two properties associated mainly because the more central members are better able to influence group opinion toward their own opinions (Propositions 10 and 11)? Before examining these (mutually compatible) alternatives, let us look at one further study, by Shaw and associates (1957), since it suggests an additional relevant consideration.

The study made use of a communications net. The pattern created in this case was a "Y," there being one central participant linked to each of three other, peripheral participants, none of whom was linked to anyone else. Each subject heard through earphones a number of easily counted clicks; the number heard was discussed among them; and each then gave his estimate of how many clicks had actually occurred. Subjects in different positions, however, heard different numbers of clicks. Three variations were used:

Condition I: Only the central subject heard a different number;

Condition II: The central subject and one peripheral subject heard more or less clicks than the other two subjects;

Condition III: Only one of the peripheral subjects heard a different number of clicks.

The results and the experimenters' comments follow:

"In both Condition I and III the deviator changed her estimate much more frequently than did the nondeviators. The central deviator did not differ from the peripheral deviator in this respect. However, the central deviator apparently did spend more time trying to get the others to agree with her than did the peripheral deviator, and the fact that the peripheral nondeviators in Condition I changed significantly more than did their counterparts in Condition III indicates that she may have had some measure of success. The effect of position within the communication net upon frequency of change of estimate is shown more clearly in Condition II in which both the central S and the peripheral S who agreed with her changed significantly less frequently than did the others in the group. It appears that the S in the more central position attempted to use her position to get others to agree with her estimate, but if the opposition became too great, she changed as frequently as did Ss in the peripheral positions" (*ibid.*, p. 327).

Shaw and his colleagues also state:

"One central S reported to the peripheral Ss that others had agreed with her own estimate, when actually they had not. In this case, all the peripheral Ss changed their estimate to agree with that of the central S" (*ibid.*).

Let us now sort these possibilities into various patterns. There are three status-properties being considered, centrality, conformity, and influence. Centrality implies both (Propositions 4 and 10), and influence and conformity imply each other (Propositions 9 and 11). Consequently, we have the following triad:

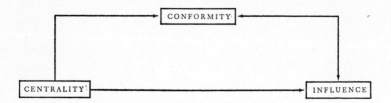

The explanation of Proposition 10 includes reference to observability, however (Propositions 2 and 8); observability is also mutually implicated with conformity (Propositions 6 and 7); and the importance of the greater observability of the central participant in the study by Shaw, et al. is evident from their account. The drawing therefore becomes somewhat more complicated:

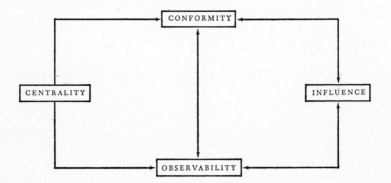

Now, from centrality four paths may lead to influence. One proceeds via conformity, which results in the exercise of influence through exemplifying or expressing common sentiments.

(Observability presumably results from conformity.) Thus:

Route 1

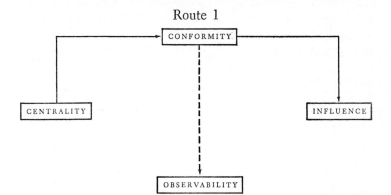

A second proceeds to conformity, but turns here toward observability: An issue comes up, the central member reflects on it, and in virtue of his own conformity correctly gauges the tenor of group opinion. He then suggests the ideas that are most acceptable, thus exercising influence and by doing so increasing his conformity as well:[6]

Route 2

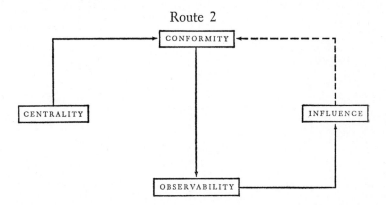

[6] This would appear to be how Rousseau felt groups should in general arrive at decisions:

"As long as several men in assembly regard themselves as a single body, they have only a single will which is concerned with their common preservation and general well-being. In this case, all the springs of

A third proceeds via observability. The influence that is exercised in this case is more consciously wielded and occurs through actions that revise the state of consensus. This leads around to conformity because group opinion on the matter has become congruent with the central member's opinion (Proposition 11). Thus:

Route 3

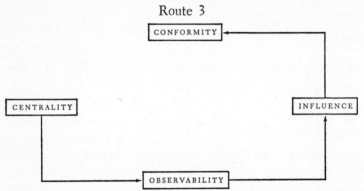

Shaw and associates suggest yet a fourth route: If the central person cannot alter consensus, he changes his own opinion and so conforms. Figuratively, he gets to observability, but then turns left up to conformity, where, by accepting and then espousing the opinion he has observed to be generally held, he turns right down to influence:

Route 4

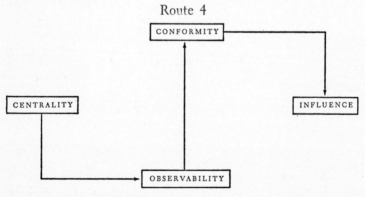

the State are vigorous and simple and its rules clear and luminous;

These patterns describe core mechanisms in the theory of influence presented here. It is through them, in conjunction with the rank-centrality relationship, that rank leads to the exercise of influence. Centrality, observability, and conformity are thus intervening variables in quite specific ways, and anything that disturbs these relationships disturbs the relation leading from rank to influence.

But what evidence supports the conjectures that such patterns exist and that they play the role attributed to them? Besides the indirectly relevant data adduced so far, practically none. The analysis here has proceeded beyond the point where previously done studies are likely to contain pertinent factual materials. Not only is the time-sequence of the variations usually obscure in existing reports, but, as earlier comments indicate, the more common measurement procedures may preclude, by their asumptions, the possibility that one or another of the patterns will appear among the findings.

The description of the four "routes" or patterns, then, is about as far as the analysis can be carried at the present time. There is evidence that the four properties are positively related and tend to vary together. And the relationships among them seem to be of the kinds described. But little more than that can be said or assumed until evidence bearing on the existence and relative frequency of the patterns is in hand. One would, indeed, prefer that such evidence were already in hand. As Homans has said, "No theory can be more sophisticated than the facts with which it deals" (1950, p. 40). On the other hand, it is sometimes useful,

---

. . . the common good is everywhere clearly apparent, and only good sense is needed to perceive it. . . .

"A State so governed needs very few laws; and, as it becomes necessary to issue new ones, the necessity is universally seen. The first man to propose them merely says what all have already felt, and there is no question of factions or intrigues or eloquence in order to secure the passage into law of what everyone has already decided to do, as soon as he is sure that the rest will act with him." (*The Social Contract*, Book IV, Chapter 1.)

as Merton has aptly if unintentionally replied, to break out of the narrow "framework of fact that happens to be at hand, even if . . . [this] means leaving demonstrated fact for acknowledged conjecture" (Lazarsfeld and Merton, 1954, p. 29).

In the third and concluding part of the chapter, to which we turn next, the derived hypothesis, that rank leads to influence, is briefly discussed and some evidence bearing on it is presented. Then the reciprocal hypothesis, that influence leads to rank, is examined. Finally, in order to complete the circle of propositions and important derivations, findings bearing on the derived hypothesis that centrality implies rank are reviewed.

Part III

13. *For any member of a small group, the higher his rank, the greater his influence.*

Proposition 13 is rooted in the theory of authority, particularly in the argument from legitimacy, although special versions of it are not uncommon in other contexts. For example, there is the very important statement by Homans (1950), whose work underlies much of the present essay, that "the sentiments of the leaders of a group carry greater weight than those of the followers in establishing a social ranking" (p. 181)—that is, in influencing consensus concerning who ranks where. Since the proposition is commented upon in several places below, it is enough here to present a few pertinent findings.

The research by Torrance (1955) on three-man bomber crews offers some evidence relevant to the hypothesis. Influence was measured by comparing individually and collectively written stories about a conference scene and deciding, on the basis of content, which members had influenced the crew's story most and least. The results over the 62 crews are as follows:[7]

	Influence			
Rank	High	Medium	Low	Total
Pilots	36	15	11	62
Navigators	23	17	22	62
Gunners	0	14	48	62

In a discussion concerning survival in enemy territory, self-ratings on influence were highly correlated with rank: 42 percent of the pilots, 9 percent of the navigators, and none of the gunners felt they had "the most influence" on the crew's final decision.

Talland's study (1954), referred to earlier, also contains data relevant to the hypothesis. Rank here is indicated by a composite "leadership" score formed from scores on public popularity, dominance (a rating on influence), and leadership (a rating on just that). The six groups for which data are available were psychotherapy groups having from 5 to 8 members. Influence appears to be measured by comparisons between pre-discussion individual rankings of topics according to their usefulness in psychotherapy groups and post-discussion group rankings. Talland shows that before the discussion, the "leader" in each group ranked the topics in a way that differed from the way most of the others ranked them but that the post-discussion group ranking corresponded very closely to the "leader's" initial ranking. (The highest-ranking participant, the psychotherapist, was not included in the measurements.)

----

[7] The data are calculated from percentages in Torrance (1955, p. 487). There is apparently some slight error in the table, and so these figures may be off by a case or two. That navigators do not bunch in the middle but tend to exercise either much or little influence reflects, I imagine, the heterogeneity of the category that results from some of them being officers with higher military rank than their pilots and others being officers with lower military rank than their pilots.

:

A study by Hare (1953) of the effects of size on interaction patterns shows a correlation between rank and influence. There were nine groups of size 5. Rank had two degrees, leader and follower, the leaders having been chosen "on the basis of recommendations by their camp counselors as boys who had leadership experience, held positions of responsibility in their (Boy Scout) troop, and were recognized as leaders by their peers." Influence in this case is indicated by the correlation between an individual's pre-interaction ranking of items for a camping trip and the group's ranking. For the leaders the mean r was .77 and for the followers, .56.

Since this hypothesis, that rank leads to influence, derives from the rank-centrality and centrality-influence hypotheses, it is of more than passing interest to note the following:

In Hare's study the association between rank and influence holds up only for active leaders (of the sort described earlier). The passive leaders, who by instruction were not central participants, had a corresponding correlation coefficient that was lower than the coefficient for their followers ($r = .50$ vs. $.55$).

The same results do *not* occur in the Preston-Heintz study (1953), after which Hare's was modeled. There appear to be two reasons for this. First, in their groups the "leaders" were not, as they were in Hare's groups, markedly higher-ranking than the other members in their respective groups but were peers, chosen for the purpose of the experiment. The students in a large college class were divided into 18 groups (of four to five members each), and each group "elected" one of their number to serve as the "leader." Second, the distribution of task-relevant knowledge appears to have offset the tenuous rank-centrality relation. The task was to rank 12 men in order of their desirability as President of the United States. Of the subjects under active leadership, only about one third afterwards named their leader as "having the greatest knowledge regarding the candidates," whereas two thirds named one or another follower. This finding was even more definite in the passively led groups, where none of the subjects named their leader as knowledgeable and 90 percent named some follower (*ibid.*, p. 581).

The Preston-Heintz study does not support the rank-influence hypothesis, then, because, first, the relative rank of the "leaders" was not, in fact, much greater than that of the followers and, second, task-relevant knowledge was not distributed according to rank differences. As a result, those designated as "leaders" were not sufficiently central relative to their followers to exercise more influence than the latter. Each of these conditions—insufficient rank differentiation and the presence of a causally relevant external factor such as information—is treated more fully in a later chapter.

In general, however, Proposition 13 is fairly well supported.

14. *For any member of a small group, the greater his influence, the higher his rank.*

A member's influence is a consequence mainly of his actions and his rank is an evaluation of him based in part on his actions. Insofar as the actions that are influential are also actions that are judged by members to be good, valuable, worth while, etc., there would be an association between rank and influence, independently of whether or not the actions were perceived to be influential. Of the various kinds of influential actions, those that tend to affect rank the most in this way are the behaviorally conforming actions that reinforce consensus by exemplifying common norms or expressing common sentiments. This proposition is thus in part a special case of what Zetterberg has called the Homans Postulate (Zetterberg, 1957, pp. 194-195; Homans, 1950, *passim*; Riecken and Homans, 1954, pp. 789-790). A variant on this interpretation of the assertion is obtained by linking the exercise of influence to rank through its effect on conformity ("Route 3" above): In virtue of moving the group's consensus closer to his own norms, a member's actions become in fact more in accord with group norms than they were and, to the extent that rank is based on evaluations of performance, his rank increases. It should be noted, however, that since the attribution of influence is in terms of effects the causes of which may not be highly visible to participants, exercising the kind of influence that changes the state of consensus carries no necessary implications for one's rank.

The hypothesis is a familiar one and is supported by findings from several studies. The findings pertain to the negative form of the hypothesis (which, strictly speaking, is the negation of Proposition 13).

A study by French (1953) of naval recruits during training provides data in support of the high-deviance/low-rank hypothesis (although the units here may not be small groups in the sense defined earlier). Deviance is indicated by the number of demerits a man received for disciplinary offenses. Rank is measured by the number of mentions a man received in answer to three nomination-questions (one concerned companions to go on liberty with; one, persons to go with on a dangerous mission; and one, persons to fill the position of Acting Chief Petty Officer, the highest-ranking position open to recruits in training). In order to control for the effects of disciplinary offenses on initial ratings, the investigator singled out from his sample the 117 recruits who received demerits only after initial ratings had been made. From those who received no demerits, he chose another 117 matched with the first on initial ratings. The mean number of mentions received by the men in the latter sample increased by about one third over the training period, whereas the mean number received by those who had deviated remained about the same.

Deviance	Initial Rating	Final Rating
No demerits	9.63	12.72
Some demerits	9.67	9.56

Kahn and Katz (1953), reviewing mainly Michigan studies on "leadership practices in relation to productivity and morale," note the following: Supervisors of high-producing sections spend more time in supervisory work and less in "straight production work" than do supervisors of low-producing sections; "in the low sections there was more frequently some one member who 'spoke up for the men when they wanted something' "; in low-producing sections, this happened about twice as often (one third of the time where ascertained) as in high-producing sections; by inference, then, the supervisors who failed to supervise (deviance) found that others were accorded a higher rank than before, which thereby diminished theirs relatively.

Studying the "sharing" of leadership in small decision-making groups, Berkowitz (1955) reports on members' reactions to conference leaders' failures to lead. If we can assume that "satisfaction with decisions arrived at, satisfaction with the leader, satisfaction with the group's process . . . [all] highly interrelated ratings" indicate that conference leaders have maintained their initially relative high rank, then Berkowitz' data support the hypothesis. For this complex "satisfaction" rating is positively associated with "leader control of procedure" (conformity) and negatively associated with such indications of leadership failure or deviance as "goal-setting by members," "solution-proposing by members," and "summarizing by members." The associations are small but consistent ($r = .3$, approximately).

A finding from Hare's research (1953) on the Boy Scout discussion groups is perhaps relevant here. It will be recalled that in the 5-man actively-led groups, the evidence indicates that the leaders were actually relatively high-ranking boys to begin with, were central during the discussions, and did exercise influence. Following the discussions Hare asked the boys to fill out a schedule that contained the question, "Who seemed to have the most influence on the group decision?" Answers to this type of question are probably a mixture of realistic evaluation and evaluation based on prior ranks (or prior proto-ranks), but if they are taken as indicators of rank, the results bear out the hypothesis, the answers being distributed as follows: "The leader"—49%; "The person with the most camping experience" —27%; "The person who talked the most"—13%; (Other)— 10% (*ibid.*, pp. 510 and 513).

15. For any member of a small group, the greater his centrality, the higher his rank.

Rank is a generalized evaluation of a member, compared with other members, and reflects group judgments about (*a*) his qualities (which here include the rank of his status, if differentiated statuses exist in the group) and (*b*) his performances (whether judged by standards commonly applied to all members or applied only to those who occupy or are candidates for his status). The extent to which a group member's rank can vary in the short run in response to variations in any other factor(s) depends on its principal components. The more it in fact results from a status-rank that is institutionalized or culturally agreed upon, the less any variations in other properties will affect it; at the extreme, a member's rank remains relatively stable no matter what he does or is like, so long as he continues to occupy the status. In the long run, perhaps, statuses that are occupied by personnel whose qualities or performances regularly fail to meet expectations are probably progessively redefined and re-ranked, but that is hardly ever possible in the short run.

Propositions such as 14 and 15, therefore, in which rank appears as a dependent variable, must be taken as pertaining primarily to groups where rank depends at least to some extent on performances or on qualities that can have varying degrees of relevance and hence be more or less valued in the short run. Ordinarily, then, the best groups for testing such propositions lack not only formally defined statuses but clearly differentiated and ranked roles of any sort other than perhaps "leader." Some of the anticipated effects on rank may show up in groups with well-defined, institutionalized role structures, as they apparently did in some of the studies just cited, but they are not likely to show up very clearly. In effect, if a group's role or status structure is clearly organized into a set of sharply ranked and, for the short run, permanently occupied positions, its larger organizational and institutional contexts are anchoring the members' ranks and preventing them from being responsive to internal variations. Such constraints contribute in an obvious way to the group's general stability, and will be discussed in terms of these functions later, but they also make such groups poor places to study the kinds of phenomena that interest us. The studies to be reviewed in support of this last proposition, then, are studies of groups organized mainly for purposes of observation and experiment, and the measures of rank in most cases are therefore measures of what was referred to earlier as "proto-rank," that is, they are members' judgments of one another's performances.

The proposition itself is a derivation from Propositions 10 and 14, which link centrality to influence and influence to rank, respectively. As will be seen, it is probably one of the best-supported general statements about small groups, and its evident validity contributes materially to the plausibility of the set of propositions as a whole.

Besides Hare's study, cited so often before and relevant here as well, there are the following:

For a set of task groups, Norfleet (1948) reports a rank-order correlation of .9 between the members' participation rates (centrality) and their being nominated as the one who "contributed most to the productivity of the group" (rank).

In a number of places positive rank-order correlations are reported between a member's participation as scored by the Bales scheme (centrality) and his being nominated as the one who "contributed the best ideas for solving the problem" or "did most to guide the discussion and keep it moving effectively" (rank). For example, Slater (1955) provides the following co-efficients:[8]

Influence Measures

Measures of Centrality	Best Ideas	Guidance
Acts initiated	.80 & .48	.75 & .51
Acts received	.74 & .44	.74 & .52

But the most convincing evidence for the causal role played by centrality in producing rank occurs in the now numerous experiments that employ Bavelas' communications-net technique, for by this method whole parts of a relational structure can be kept inactive. Leavitt's experiment (1951) is very well known, but I will nevertheless summarize it here in some detail because of its special relevance to this hypothesis.

Four types of structure were used: the circle(O), the chain or vee (V), the Y, and the wheel, star, or ex (X). Thus:

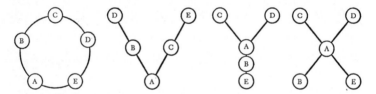

According to the earlier discussion, there are two dimensions to centrality, the number of others with whom a member is in contact (relational centrality) and the number of contacts a member has with others (interaction centrality). In the present case, what is to be shown first is that by controlling relational centrality (RC), one can also control interaction centrality (IC), at least in groups this small and of this sort. The measure of RC should take into account the relative ease with which variously located members can communicate with the other members of the group. Since all of Leavitt's groups are of the

[8] The lower correlations are for groups exhibiting low consensus on their responses to the questions on best ideas and guidance. See, for similar results, Bales (1952, p. 154; 1953, pp. 145-147); and Borgatta (1954).

same size (namely, 5), we need only count, for each position, the minimal number of relations linking it to all other positions. For example, in the O-type, any one position is one relation removed from two adjacent positions and two relations removed from the other two positions, giving it a score of 6. In the Y-type, position C is one relation removed from positions A, B, and D and two from position E, giving C a score of 5, and so on. For IC, we must use acts initiated because Leavitt reports only the mean number of messages sent from each position. These were totaled in order to have a base figure for each net. Within a net, the average number of messages sent by positions having the same degree of relational centrality was computed, and this average, divided by the base figure for the net, gave the percentages used below as the measure of interaction centrality.

Net	Positions	Relational Centrality	Interaction Centrality
O	A-E	6	20%
V	A	6	30%
	B & C	7	25%
	D & E	10	10%
Y	A	5	36%
	B	6	29%
	C & D	8	12%
	E	9	12%
X	A	4	48%
	B-E	7	13%
All		4	48%
		5	36%
		6	26%
		7	17%
		8	12%
		9	12%
		10	10%

In summary, then, the experimenter creates varying degrees of interaction centrality by manipulating the degrees of relational centrality. Parallel results are reported for almost all experiments on communications nets of these types. See, for example, Heise and Miller (1955, p. 360); Shaw et al. (1957); and Berkowitz (1957).

The next step is to show that differences in rank result from the created differences in centrality. In this case, the rank of a position is presumed to be reflected by the proportion of possible votes its incumbents received in answer to the question, "Did your group have a leader and if so, who?" I have averaged the votes for positions of similar degrees of centrality within the same type of net.

Net	RC	IC:%	(a) No. of Positions	(b) Base = 25 × (a)	(c) Votes Rec'd	(d) % of Votes: c/b
O	6	20	5	125	14	11%
V	6	30	1	25	12	48%
	7	25	2	50	6	12
	10	10	2	50	0	0
Y	5	36	1	25	17	68%
	6	29	1	25	1	4
	8	12	2	50	2	4
	9	12	1	25	0	0
X	4	48	1	25	23	92%
	7	13	4	100	0	0

The comparison remains here within each kind of net. But one can see from the table that as the experimenter increased the centralization of a group, by altering the kind of net used, the distribution of rank altered also, becoming less diffuse as the centralization increased.

A replication by Goldberg (1955) permits us to check on these results. In this study ten groups were used in each of three nets, V, Y, and X. The connection over nets between centralization and the distribution of rank was not observed; but the correlation between centrality and rank among positions within a net is again obvious.

Net	RC	(a) No. of Positions	(b) Base = 50 × (a)	(c) Votes Rec'd	(d) % of Votes c/b
V	6	1	50	10	20%
	7	2	100	16	16
	10	2	100	7	7
Y	5	1	50	21	42%
	6	1	50	5	10
	8	2	100	3	3
	9	1	50	4	8
X	4	1	50	16	32%
	7	4	200	13	6.5

Summary

The chapter having been long and the issues covered diverse, I will keep the summary brief and merely list below the 15 statements, the sources of the six which are derivations, and a qualitative comment after each regarding the direct evidence bearing on it. As can be seen, all but three of the assertions have "some" support in fact and four are fairly well supported.

Proposition		Variables	Source	Direct Evidence
I.	1.	Rank-Centrality		Good
	2.	Centrality-Observability		Some
	3.	Rank-Observability	(1,2)	Some
	4.	Centrality-Conformity		Some
	5.	Rank-Conformity	(1,4)	Some
II.	6.	Observability-Conformity		Good
	7.	Conformity-Observability		Some
	8.	Observability-Influence		None
	9.	Conformity-Influence		None
	10.	Centrality-Influence	(2,8;4,9)	Good
	11.	Influence-Observability	(12,7)	None
	12.	Influence-Conformity		Some

III.	13.	Rank-Influence	(1,4,9)	Some
	14.	Influence-Rank		Some
	15.	Centrality-Rank	(4,9,14;2,8,14)	Good

In the next chapter some additional empirical materials are presented, as well as some limitations on the scope of the assertions.

[4]

Two Applications

The conceptualization and set of propositions examined in the preceding chapters can be put to several uses. For present purposes three are distinguished.

If one takes the several propositions collectively, the simplest general derivation is that the five properties imply one another and tend to be associated at any given time. Those in a group who are the highest-ranking are likely as well to be the most central and the most conforming, to have the highest observability and to exercise the most influence. Such a conjunction of structural characteristics would seem to fit what is sometimes meant by "leadership," and the first part of this chapter briefly discusses that concept. Since other properties besides these have been attributed to leaders, the discussion provides an opportunity to consider some of the factors that are relevant to the exercise of influence but are not treated systematically in the present essay.

Another way of using the basic ideas is to view them as describing sequential relations among the variables over time. In this view, centrality "leads to" influence not only in the sense that it implies influence logically but also in the sense that those who are the most central at one point in time are likely to be the most influential at some subsequent point in time (regardless of their degree of initial influence). The second part of the chapter draws on material from a recently completed study to illustrate how the basic ideas may be used in this way to analyze developmental sequences, in this case the development of influence structures in groups that formed units of a training program.

A third way to interpret the ideas is to view them as depicting a process basic to the interaction system of small groups. Two principal substantive assumptions are introduced in this interpretation. One is analogous to that introduced into theories of authority that use the concept of legitimacy: The distribution of influence among the members of a group is stable if it is legitimate, which in the present context can be taken to mean, if it parallels the distribution of rank. Two, there is a tendency toward legitimacy in groups, that is, toward parallel distributions of rank and influence over the members. The set of concepts and propositions can then be viewed as catching up the main elements of the cyclical process that reflects this tendency and is responsible for the conjunction of rank and influence. The ideas are interpreted in this way in the following chapter.

Notes on Leadership

Structural Properties of Leaders

The ideas in the preceding two chapters may be used descriptively to define leadership, in which case the concept is structural in content and the leaders of a group are those highest on the five properties of rank, centrality, observability, conformity, and influence. Some implications of this formulation are explored shortly, but first an example of this use of the properties may prove helpful. Whyte's concluding description of Doc in relation to the rest of the Nortons provides a case in point.

Centrality plays a large part in Whyte's description of "the men with top positions," the leaders:

> "The leader is the focal point for the organization of his group. In his absence, the members of the gang are divided into a number of small groups. . . . When the leader appears . . . the small units form into one large group. The conversation becomes general, and unified action frequently follows. The leader becomes the central point in the discussion" (Whyte, 1943 p. 258).

Or, again:

> "This discussion should not give the impression that the leader is the only man who proposes a course of action. Other men frequently have ideas, but their suggestions must go through the proper channels if they are to go into effect" (*ibid.*, p. 261).

Again:

> "Doc was accustomed to a high frequency of interaction with the members of his group . . . While he sometimes directly originated action in set events for the group, it was customary for one of the other members to originate action for him in a pair event, and then he would originate action in a set event. That is, someone would suggest a course of action, and then Doc would get the boys together and organize group activity" (*ibid.*, p. 266).

Observability is coupled with centrality:

> "The followers look to him for advice and encouragement, and he receives more of their confidences than any other man. Consequently, he knows more about what is going on in the group than anyone else" (*ibid.*, p. 259).

Whyte does not mention *conformity* as that concept has been used here, but several kinds of *influence* are present. *Behavioral conformity* and its reinforcement effects on consensus are linked directly to *rank*:

> "Not all corner boys live up to their obligations equally well, and this factor partly accounts for the differentiation of status among them [of rank, in our terms]. The man with a low status may violate his obligations without much change in his position. His fellows know that he has failed to discharge certain obligations in the past, and his position reflects his past performances. On the other hand, the leader is depended upon by all the members to meet his personal obligations. He cannot fail to do so without causing confusion and endangering his position" (*ibid.*, p. 257).

With respect to *innovative influence*, which entails introducing new ideas into the group's consensus, there is the following statement:

> "The leader is the man who acts when the situation requires action. He is more resourceful than his followers. Past ideas have shown that his ideas were right. In this sense 'right' simply means satisfactory to the members. He is the most independent in judgment. While the followers are undecided as to a course of action or upon the character of a newcomer, the leader makes up his mind" (*ibid.*, p. 259).

The exercise of influence through *adjudication* is also mentioned:

> "Whenever there is a quarrel among the boys, he hears of it almost as soon as it happens. Each party to the quarrel may appeal to him to work out a solution . . ." (*ibid.*)

There is also the influence that is exercised through acting on the area of consensus concerning who occupies what positions:

> "A man's standing depends partly upon the leader's belief that he has been conducting himself properly" (*ibid.*).

:

Writers have of course attributed to leaders many other characteristics besides these, but one in particular is basic to leadership as a structural concept, namely, its definition by participants as a distinctive status or role in the group.

If high rank in the Nortons was associated with high centrality and influence, that was so at least partly because specific normative expectations provided for the association: "The members *do not feel* that the gang is really gathered until the leader appears. They *recognize an obligation* to wait for him before beginning any group activity, and when he is present they *expect* him to make decisions" (*ibid.*, p. 258, emphasis added). Another specific obligation mentioned by Whyte relates to the leader's exercise of influence through adjudication: "Whereas there may be hard feeling among some of the followers, the leader cannot bear a grudge against any man in the group" (*ibid.*, p. 259). Another has to do with relations with other groups: "Whether the relationship is one of conflict, competition, or cooperation, he is expected to represent the interests of his fellows" (*ibid.*, p. 260). In short, not only was the highest-ranking member factually the most central, the most influential, and so on, but also, the group members distinguished clearly between the member who was the highest-ranking, most central, etc., and the rest; and they defined in a distinctive way their relations with him and his with them.

Leadership in small groups, can, then, be made into an explanatory concept by using it to refer to a particular kind of institutionalized role, one that through its constituent expectations and behaviors tends to bring about the conjunction of the five properties, at least at their upper extremes. Used in this way, the concept refers to what is probably the simplest and the most common mechanism by which parallel distributions of the properties are generated and maintained. As Whyte says:

Each member of the corner gang has his own position in the gang structure. Although the positions may remain unchanged over long periods of time, they should not be conceived in static terms. To have a position means that the individual has a customary way of interacting with other members of the group . . . *The group is organized around the men with top positions* . . . (*ibid.*, pp. 262-263, emphasis added).

The content of the role of course can and does vary considerably.

The properties are mutually related, however, independently of specific kinds of leadership roles or of the institutionalization of leadership generally. The existence of the role (or status) in a group only makes it more likely than it would otherwise be that the relationships among the properties will in fact occur. A leader is one who, in virtue of distinctive rights and responsibilities attaching to his membership, is more likely than others in the group to be high on all five properties, that is, to combine the attributes of high rank, high centrality, and so on. Moreover, if groups with and without an institutionalized leadership role (or status) are compared, the high ranking members of the first are more likely than the high-ranking members of the second to be high as well on centrality, observability, conformity, and influence.

The tendency for these properties to be associated, and the facilitating effect which the existence of a leadership role has on the tendency, are countered by the dependence of each property upon numerous factors lying outside a group's interaction system and in one or another of its environments. The specific nature of these causally relevant external factors differs from group to group, depending upon the particular environments. Whyte's description, however, suggests several that probably have a fairly general relevance.

It is probably true for most groups, for example, that "the leader's reputation outside the group tends to support his standing within the group, and his position in the group supports his reputation among outsiders" (*ibid.*, p. 260). Or, more precisely, since this statement contains two distinct kinds of dependence, a member's relative rank within a group is causally related to (a) the rank that non-members treat him as having within the group and (b) the ranks he is accorded within his other membership groups.

Centrality seems to be peculiarly subject to variations caused by external factors. It is perhaps always affected by variations in motivation (which is viewed here as located in the interaction system's psychological environment); although, owing to its including both overt acts initiated and overt acts received, a group can maintain the relative centrality of a member at a given level despite fairly wide variations in his motivation to take part actively. The high centrality of a leader, for example, whose motivation to participate actively drops for some reason, can be maintained, at least in the short run, if the members increase the number of acts he receives. Sometimes these causally relevant variations in motivation occur alone, but often they occur in conjunction with variations in other kinds of factors.

Whyte accounts as follows for the breakdown of leadership in the Nortons, that is, for their failure to keep combined in the occupant of the leadership status the attributes of high rank, high centrality, etc. He relates a reduced flow of money to the leader, a certain amount of which was required if Doc was to comply with expectations, to a lowering of Doc's motivation to participate, and through that to a reduction of his centrality. Earlier Whyte had pointed out descriptively that "the leader spends more money on his followers than they on him" (*ibid.*, p. 258), and the context of the discussion makes it clear that this pattern reflected a normative expectation. Then, later on, he says of Doc: "Lacking money, he could not participate in group activities without accepting the support of others and letting them determine his course of action. Therefore, on many occasions he avoided associating with his friends—that is, his frequency of interaction was drastically reduced" (*ibid.*, p. 266).

:

Variations in centrality, although frequently a function of variations in motivation, may nevertheless take place independently, through variations in the flow of relevant "facilities," (see Parsons, 1951, pp. 119-127). This general point is illustrated in an experiment by Shaw (1954), who used communication nets in order to study the effects on centrality of varying distributions of relevant information.

Participants were required to solve problems, each of which consisted of piecing together eight items of information. In the control condition the four positions of a net received two items each, while in the experimental condition, position A (see diagram) received five of the items and the other positions each received one. The nets were constructed as follows:

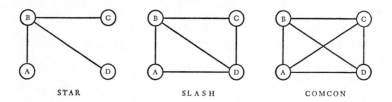

The following table summarizes the results. Although the differences are not large, A's relative participation increased in each case:

A's proportion of the total participation under two conditions in three types of communication net.

	Condition		
Net	Equal Information		A Has Most Information
Star	15%	vs.	23%
Slash	22%	vs.	26%
Comcon	24%	vs.	28%

What Whyte's analysis and Shaw's results suggest is that the distribution of facilities affects specifically the rank-centrality relationship. If they are distributed among members other than in accordance with their rank, the degree of association between rank and centrality is presumably less than it would otherwise be. The normative patterns governing the introduction of facilities into a group's interaction system are thus highly relevant to the structuring of influence, as the following excerpt, again from Whyte but this time about a gang called the Millers, illustrates:

> Sam Franco, the leader, was out of work except for an occasional odd job; yet whenever he had a little money, he spent it on Joe and Chichi, his closest friends, who were next to him in the structure of the group. When Joe or Chichi had money, which was less frequent, they reciprocated. Sam frequently paid for two members who stood close to the bottom of his group and occasionally for others. The two men who held positions immediately below Joe and Chichi were considered very well off according to Cornerville standards. *Sam said that he occasionally borrowed money from them, but never more than fifty cents at a time.* Such loans he repaid at the earliest possible moment. There were four other members with lower positions in the group, *who nearly always had more money than Sam. He did not recall ever having borrowed from them.* He said that the only time he had obtained a substantial sum from anyone around his corner was when he borrowed eleven dollars from a friend who was the *leader* of another corner gang.
>
> The situation was the same among the Nortons. Doc did not hesitate to accept money from Danny, but he avoided taking any money from the followers (Whyte, 1943, pp. 257-258; emphasis added).

Moreover, as the example of Sam's borrowing from another corner boy leader indicates, the observed tendency for leaders to make and to maintain contacts with other groups,[1] and the paral-

---

[1] This tendency has been observed many times. See, for specific instances, besides Whyte (1943), Roethlisberger and Dickson (1939), pp. 382-383, 464-465; and Horsfall and Arensberg, 1949, pp. 13-28. The general point is made in Homans (1950), pp. 185-186, and in Katz and Lazarsfeld (1955), pp. 123-130.

lel normative expectations to this effect mentioned earlier, bear directly on the introduction of facilities, which generally originate outside the group, into the system. Not only do social relations with outsiders affect rank, then, but, through their significance for access to or control over facilities, they affect centrality as well.

It is not the point of these comments to develop a "theory of leadership" but merely to indicate how the ideas in the preceding chapters can be used in an analysis of leadership structures. For this purpose it has seemed sufficient to show that one of the best-known analyses of this sort proceeds as if the concepts and propositions of this essay constituted its theoretical framework.

We now take up briefly two matters often raised in discussions of leaders, first, the issue of their conformity versus their innovative effects, and after that, the question of their "popularity."

Kinds of Influence Exercised by Leaders

The question is sometimes posed whether leaders conform more or innovate more than other members. It seems on occasion that "conformity," in these discussions, refers to behavior in accord with norms and "innovation" to behavior divergent from norms—that is, to deviant behavior. The issue posed is thus at times an artifact of the assumption that all behavior is normatively defined, which is seldom a warranted assumption.

If this assumption is avoided, one can classify actions into three broad categories, compliance (behavior in accord with group norms), deviance (behavior explicitly counter to norms), and noncompliance (behavior that is neither clearly compliant nor clearly deviant). Each of these, viewed with respect to their effects on consensus, can be phrased in terms of influence. Patterns of compliance, as has been said, have a reinforcing effect. Patterns of deviance have no effect; they are specifically uninfluential, indicating the tendency to anomie (as a state of a group's consensus). Patterns of noncompliance tend to result in norm formation, the guiding idea or sentiment moving first to the periphery of consensus, then to being near-normative, then to being normative, as the particular pattern is continually repeated.

Translated into these terms, the question asks about the kinds of influence leaders exercise. First, clearly, there is no necessary conflict between "conformity" and "innovation": relative to the other members, the leader of a group may be most influential in both respects, both complying more than others to existing norms and introducing more new ideas into the group's consensus than others do; at the same time, he presumably evidences less deviance, though this is perhaps not so clear and will be discussed shortly.

Second, however, it seems likely that, as between the two kinds of influence, most leaders of most small groups exercise far more influence through reinforcing existing normative elements than through introducing new ones. That is, at any given time they behave in ways that accord with existing norms to a far greater extent than in ways that are not (as yet) normatively defined; or, at the level of discourse, their expressed opinions and sentiments more often reiterate received ideas than introduce new ones. The main reason for this probably lies in their high conformity and high observability. Their own greater commitment to the shared norms, coupled with their greater awareness of group expectations, makes it likely that they will devote much effort simply to reinforcing or heightening others' commitments—that is, to maintaining consensus intact or increasing the normativeness of the main ideas and sentiments it contains.

It remains generally true, nevertheless, that, as Whyte suggests, "the leader is the man who acts when the situation requires action" (1943, p. 259). That is, to repeat the main point, although most of the influence a leader exercises is in support of existing norms, if new ideas or sentiments become normative, he will have been the one who, more than anyone else, is responsible for having introduced them. For no matter who initially suggests a "new idea," it is not moved into the group's consensus, and certainly not into the normative sphere, unless continually supported and reinforced. And the leader's support is almost always critical, since if he supports it, others are likely to support it as well. They will follow him not so much because "past events have shown that his ideas were right" (*ibid.*), which suggests a more instrumental view than most small group members probably take. Rather, the most general reason behind the trial acceptance of a new idea advanced by a leader is that each member's standing in the group is in large part a reflection of his, the leader's, expressed evaluation—he influences consensus on rankings more than others do—and his response to another member in public is positive, on the average, in the degree to which the other agrees with him. That "past events have shown that his ideas were right" points to his influence and its more or less direct effects on his rank; but it is his rank, and the consequent weight of his sanctions, that gains the members' initial behavioral compliance with a new idea. After that, its movement toward becoming normative depends mainly on his continuous reinforcement of it.

With respect to deviant behavior, which by definition here is noninfluential and so is unrelated to the question posed, its significance for leadership lies on a completely different plane. Deviance might seem to have effects on centrality, and for that reason a brief digression is justified. As the well-known experiment by Schachter (1953) on the rejection of deviates illustrates, visible deviant behavior or opinions, particularly if persistent, can have a decided effect on patterns of communication. If visible deviance varied inversely with rank, its frequent occurrence would probably affect the rank-centrality relation, since the lowest-ranking members would, apparently, be more central than was consistent with their rank. It may be doubted, however, that deviance very often seriously affects the relationship.

First, a low-ranking member, when he overtly acts, may be more likely to deviate visibly than a high-ranking member when he acts. But the former usually takes an active part in affairs so much less often than the high-ranking member that his portion of the group's total of visibly deviant actions is probably on the average not much larger than the latter's.

Moreover, as Schachter's data show, there are limits to the amount of activity that is devoted to the control of deviance. These limits probably reflect the same tendency that in part underlies the rank-centrality relation, that of allotting acts received by members according to their rank. At some point in the control of deviance, more attention comes to be paid to a low-ranking deviant than his rank justifies, that is, than he is worth in the members' eyes. After this point, the curve of communications to him drops off. He may simply be ignored, which (in time) amounts to the development of differential obligations with respect to basic membership norms. In the Nortons, "the man with a low status may violate his obligations without much change in his position. His fellows know that he has failed to discharge certain obligations in the past, and his position reflects his past performances" (Whyte, 1943, p. 257). Or, the membership boundaries of the group may be redrawn to exclude him, which is the ultimate sanction available to most small groups. There is, though, a third possibility: If the group strongly values maintaining the existing membership intact and as equals, the ideas or sentiments that define the behavior as deviant may in time cease to be normative, owing to the tolerance of their repeated violation.

Finally, it is usually the case that those who respond to the deviance are the high-ranking members, and their degree of centrality is thus not seriously affected. Schachter, it will be recalled, was himself the leader in his groups, and it is a basic condition of his results that he "took no part in the discussion except to answer the few questions directed to him" (1953, p. 225).

In summary, then, the net effect of deviance on the rank-centrality relation is probably not large. Only if its incidence becomes extraordinarily high would it disturb the relation. But then, it would disturb much else besides, and the reason for the disturbance would be related more to the failure of the influence process than to a shift in the patterning of interaction *per se*.

Popularity

The leader of a group is sometimes defined as the most popular or the best-liked member. Alternatively, feelings of "liking" and "disliking" are sometimes held to affect patterns of interaction and hence the location of centrality. Since these relationships among centrality, liking, and rank appear to be quite complex, the following remarks can at best touch on one or two of the more critical issues.

It will be useful to have in mind two alternative pictures of group structures and processes. In one the units are, as they have been so far, the members, who exhibit certain properties which in turn are related to one another logically. In the other, the units are the substantive social relations between pairs of members. The group in the latter case appears to be a network of such intermember relations, the members being merely the points at which the threads of the network intersect. The social relations are then considered analytically: properties are attributed to them and the group is analyzed into as many kinds of networks as there are dimensions to the relations. There is a network of observable interaction, parallel to it a network of sentiments of liking and disliking, and so forth.

To begin with, we may use the relational focus and ask, How does the network of affectivity impinge on the network of interactions? Homans suggests a very specific answer: The two networks are completely congruent:

We can, then, sum up the relationship between interaction and sentiment both in the group as a whole and in the subgroups by saying once more that the more frequently persons interact with one another, the stronger their sentiments of friendship for one another are apt to be (1950, p. 133).

And:

> Persons who feel sentiments of liking for one another will express those sentiments in activities over and above the activities of the external system (*ibid.*, p. 134).

That is, interaction and positive mutual affectivity are distributed over the group's social relations in like degree. Switching now from the relations as units to the members as units, we can conclude that centrality and popularity are also distributed among the members in like degree.

Homans has also stated a version of the rank-centrality hypothesis:

> The higher a man's social rank, the larger will be the number of persons that originate interaction for him, either directly or through intermediaries (*ibid.*, 182).

And:

> The higher a man's social rank, the larger the number of persons for whom he originates interaction, either directly or through intermediaries (*ibid.*).

Consequently, members have about as much centrality as they have rank, and thus have as much rank as popularity and vice-versa. For our particular problem, this means that sentiments of liking operate to reinforce and to heighten the association between rank and centrality.

If nothing is wrong with the reasoning, surely something is with the premises. It is not even true very often, much less usually, that rank and popularity are highly associated.

Homans, recognizing this difficulty, takes another tack:

The fact is that in any group another tendency exists besides the one by which interaction flows toward a leader, and the actual relation between sentiment and interaction represents a balance between the two tendencies (*ibid.*, p. 183).

And:

The more nearly equal in social rank a number of men are, the more frequently they will interact with one another (*ibid.*, p. 184).

These statements require a return to the relational focus. They also require the introduction of a third plane, that of rank differences. The second assertion says, then, that rank differences and frequency of interaction are inversely distributed over a group's relations: the smaller the rank difference between any two members, the more often they interact together. Shifting back to our focus on members, this makes middle-ranking members the more central, and by the earlier assertion, the more popular. Or, assuming they are the more popular and that interaction follows sentiments of liking rather than rank, they become the more central. And the rank-centrality assertion does not hold up. Popularity and centrality coincide, but their relation to rank is curvilinear, not positive throughout. In such cases, feelings of liking operate to depress the association between rank and centrality, even to the point where it does not exist, or rather, to the point where it is positive over the lower-ranking half of the membership and negative over the higher-ranking half.

It would appear, then, that feelings of liking have no determinate effects on the rank-centrality relationship. Is there any theoretical reason why this might be so?

Riecken and Homans have devised a formula that may be of use here.

If the liking of one man for another varies with the "goodness" or "importance" of the other's activity, measured in terms of a group norm, and if the liking of one for the other also varies with the interaction he gives to the other, then it is reasonable to predict that the interaction he gives to the other will vary inversely as the "goodness" or "importance" of the other's activity, provided sentiment remains constant. Or, in symbolic language,

$$S_{op} = f(I_{op} . A_p),$$

where S_{op} is the liking of any member o for any member p; I_{op} is the frequency of interaction from o to p, and A_p is a measure of the "goodness" or "importance" of p's activity in terms of some group norm—the higher the score the better the activity (1954, p. 799).

"A_p," in our terms, is behavioral conformity and so a form of influence. But let us substitute rank for it, that is, the members' collective evaluation of the other member's "goodness" or "importance." In this way, degree of liking of one member o for another p (relative to o's liking for other members, i.e., o's preference for p) is a resultant of his interaction with p and p's rank. If p's rank is low, it takes a lot of interaction for o to prefer him to others, whereas if p's rank is high, a little interaction goes a long way.

Impressionistically, this seems reasonable, but it can be sharpened. It may be true that we approve of those who like us, but it is probably more often true that we like those who approve of us, and, moreover, that our degree of liking depends on the weight or importance of their approval. Let us assume that this is so, and let us assume also that what determines the weight of another's approval is his rank: His approval of us means more, the more approval he receives, and his rank represents the degree to which he is approved in the group. On these assumptions, o prefers p (likes p relative to others) in proportion to the frequency with which p expresses approval of o "times" p's rank. *It is thus not the sheer frequency of interaction between o and p that is relevant to o's liking p; it is the extent to which p's responses to o express approval of o.* The little evidence available to suggest that this may not be too wide of the mark occurs in studies employing the Bales categories. "Best-liked" men rank second or third on centrality, but, in comparison with "best-idea" men, who usually rank first, have in one study a slightly higher scored output of "positive reactions," 28 percent versus 23 percent (Slater, 1955, p. 506).

The effect of liking or popularity on the rank-centrality relationship is indeterminate within the theory, then, because the theory as formulated includes no distinctions among kinds of actions as sanctions and so cannot take into account systematically varying rates of positive or negative sanctioning. This suggests in turn, though, that the significance of popularity for leadership depends to a considerable extent on whether a group defines interpersonal affectivity as an appropriate or an inappropriate feeling. Again, normative distinctions of this sort are not systematically taken into account here.

In summary, sentiments of liking, it may be assumed, are always causally relevant to patterns of interaction, and hence in principle to centrality. Homans' formulation of this basic general orientation, in terms of the likelihood of interaction between pairs of people, states it simply and clearly. However, whether and to what extent, in specific circumstances, variations in such sentiments will be found to occasion significant variations in the distribution of centrality, and hence in the distribution of influence, depends upon a number of conditions. Among these conditions are the following.

Of most importance, perhaps, is whether such feelings are normatively appropriate guides to action in a group. The greater the commitment by participants to norms of affective neutrality, the less are such sentiments likely to have an effect on the directions of interaction *within* the group. (Those who develop mutual feelings of liking in spite of the norms may well interact increasingly outside of the group, though.) Also, given some degree of appropriateness, the signifiance of such sentiments for centrality depends on the occurrence and appropriateness of *preferences*, of some members being liked more than others. Normative elements are again relevant, the basic question being whether preferences are permitted or whether the normative emphasis, so far as sentiments of liking are concerned, is on solidarity through equality: each member may be enjoined to like all others and to about the same extent, since all are equally members.

In groups where sentiments of preference are felt to be legitimate or are encouraged, the critical question concerns whether the distribution of "popularity" coincides with the distribution of rank. As was said, this seems to depend mainly on the relative frequency of positive sanctioning by the higher-ranking members. The less often they engage in negative sanctioning relative to others, the less likely it is that sentiments of liking are displaced onto somewhat lower-ranking members. Also relevant is the group's over-all form of inter-action and its norms pertaining to participation in set events, since the two structure the opportunities available for expressing sentiments of differential liking through differential rates of initiating actions to others. In general, the more often inter-action takes the form of set events, or the stronger the norms proscribing by-play during set events, the less are preferences likely to affect the rank-centrality relation.

So far as the present theory is concerned, this listing of conditions suggests viewing popularity, or sentiments of liking, much as motivation to participate and access to facilities is viewed, as factors that are causally relevant to influence through their effects on centrality, but that lie outside the narrowly circumscribed boundaries of the basic interaction system of small groups.

Summary

Using the ideas from the preceding chapters, this section has suggested an approach to the study of leaders and leadership structures, has reviewed in these terms Whyte's well-known analysis of corner-boy leaders, and has discussed the questions of innovation *versus* conformity and of popularity. The aim has been both to indicate the relevance of the ideas to topics of general interest and to illustrate how certain factors, although not viewed as "within" a group's interaction system, may nevertheless be taken into account in particular analyses. The same double aim informs the second section of the chapter, to which we next turn, but the particular use to which the ideas are put is different.

The Influence Process in a Training Program

In this section the body of concepts and propositions developed earlier is interpreted as describing the developmental sequences through which a structuring of influence comes about. The data are drawn from a larger study which examines various features of a training program in order to determine whether and to what extent each contributes to the program's measured effectiveness.[2] At the time the study was being designed, the outlines of the theory had been worked out but with reference to the exercise of authority in complex organizations, and its relevance to the problem of the research was not clearly seen until after the analysis was begun. In consequence, the fit between concepts and indicators is only moderately good at best, but it is sufficient to illustrate the use of the theory in this kind of analysis.

In 1958, when the study was conducted, the program (or "encampment") was attended by 101 young men and women, ranging in age from 17 to 24 and drawn from all parts of the country and all major ethnic groups, religions, and social

[2] Terence K. Hopkins with the assistance of Sanci Michael, *Group Structure and Opinion Change*, New York: Bureau of Applied Social Research, 1963. This study grew out of a complex evaluation of the program, the results of which are reported in Herbert H. Hyman, Charles R. Wright, and Terence K. Hopkins, *Applications of Methods of Evaluation: Four Studies of the Encampment for Citizenship*, Berkeley and Los Angeles: The University of California Press, 1962. The collection of the data reported here was supported by a grant from the Ford Foundation, and the analysis of the data, by a grant from the Council for Research in the Social Sciences, Columbia University. The assistance of both is gratefully acknowledged.

classes. Several kinds of subgroups are examined in the larger study but for present purposes data on two, the discussion groups and the dormitory groups, will prove sufficient. Upon arriving at the encampment each participant (or "camper") was assigned both to a dormitory group and to a discussion group, the two memberships being so allocated that each person had two nonoverlapping sets of co-members. The ten dormitory groups averaged ten campers and two staff members each and the nine discussion groups, eleven campers and one staff member each. The discussion groups met regularly each morning for about an hour and a half following a general lecture. The dormitory groups did not have meetings proper, but long discussions regularly occurred in each before the members went to sleep each night.

Each of these nineteen groups started with a minimum of organization and developed a more or less well-defined structure over the course of the six weeks. The first section below describes the structure in the discussion groups at the end of the program, and the second presents some material on the processes responsible for the development. The discussion groups, as it turned out, proved to contribute directly to the program's effectiveness, but the dormitory groups did not, and the third section below examines why this was so.

The Distribution of Influence in the Discussion Groups at the End of the Program

The institution of the discussion group, with its single differentiated role of group leader, is so widespread in the American educational system that the basic norms guiding behavior in these particular groups were presumably well established in the personalities of most of the participants long before their arrival at the encampment. Two or three campers, possibly, were unfamiliar with discussion-group procedures, but there appear to have been only minor differences among the rest in their degree of normative commitment in this area.

Parallel to this sphere of consensus on discussion-group norms was the plane of interaction organized by the norms. Briefly, interaction in the groups almost always took the form of set events. Scheduled meetings were regularly held, and most members attended most of them, both absenteeism and tardiness being very low. Moreover, although staff members differed to some extent in how actively they took part in the discussions, in all nine groups the interaction centered about the discussion-group leader.

By the end of the program the distribution of influence was as we would expect it to be on the basis of the theory: Within each group, rank, centrality, conformity, and influence were all positively associated. (No adequate measures of observability were included.) Although the observations are for a single point in time (the end of the program), and hence strictly speaking can indicate only that the properties were or were not associated at that time, I shall present them as if they had been made in the sequence leading from differences in rank to differences in influence.

The properties of rank, centrality, and influence were measured by nomination questions asked on the final questionnaire. When answering these questions, participants were free to mention their staff leader; but apparently the instructions were ambiguous, for the results are inconsistent. The data used here therefore concern campers only. In order to keep the text as brief as possible, detailed descriptions of the indicators are given in an Appendix to this chapter.

Rank-Centrality (Proposition 1). The discussion-group leader is left out of these tabulations, and rank thus refers here to the campers' evaluations of one another. Whether these would have served to organize interaction in the absence of the discussion leader is open to doubt, but there is little question that by the end of the encampment, those who were the higher-ranking members of their groups were also, generally, the more central members.

Table 4.1 contains the data. Both rank and centrality are measured by nomination questions (as described in the Appendix to the chapter), the replies to which were first analyzed separately for each group and only subsequently combined as in the table. The indicators are crude, but even so, a moderately strong association between the two properties is apparent.

TABLE 4.1
RANK AND CENTRALITY IN THE DISCUSSION GROUPS

Rank	Centrality			Total	N
	High	Medium	Low		
High	49	46	5	100%	41
Medium	35	38	27	100%	26
Low	6	29	65	100%	34
Total	31	38	31	100%	101

h = Index of order association = .50 *

* See Wallis and Roberts, 1956, pp. 282-284.

Centrality-Influence (Proposition 10). An even stronger relationship is evident between centrality and influence (Table 4.2). Influence here is also measured by a nomination question, but as is discussed in the Appendix to the chapter, the replies to the question probably provide a more valid measure of influence than they may at first seem to do.

TABLE 4.2
CENTRALITY AND INFLUENCE IN THE DISCUSSION GROUPS

Centrality	Influence			Total	N
	High	Medium	Low		
High	77	3	19	99%	31
Medium	26	15	59	100%	39
Low	0	10	90	100%	31
Total	34	10	56	100%	101

h = .82

It follows from Tables 4.1 and 4.2 that a fairly strong association marks the relationship between rank and influence (Proposition 13). For the record, Table 4.3 is included here.

TABLE 4.3
RANK AND INFLUENCE IN THE
DISCUSSION GROUPS

Rank	High	Influence Medium	Low	Total	N
High	54	17	29	100%	41
Medium	35	0	65	100%	26
Low	9	9	82	100%	34
Total	34	10	56	100%	101

$h = .64$

One might expect the association in Table 4.3 on any of a number of grounds. What the theory does, however, is to make it a product of the separate associations between rank and centrality, and centrality and influence. It thus implies that centrality is a necessary link between them, in the sense that high-ranking members who are low on centrality will also be low on influence and low-ranking members who are high on centrality will also be high on influence. The data in Table 4.4 suggest that centrality did in fact play this critical intervening role in these groups. Among the 9 high- or medium-ranking members who were low on centrality, only 1 was high or medium on influence, whereas among the 11 medium- or low-ranking members who were high on centrality, 9 were high or medium on influence.

Conformity. This property plays at least two important roles in the theory, one as an intervening or conditioning variable in the relationship between centrality and influence, which is discussed now, and one as a determinant of rank, which is discussed in the next section.

Conformity here is the correspondence between a member's degree of liberalism and his discussion-group's liberalism (this area being the one in which the program intended to be and was in fact most effective). Details on the measurement procedures are given in the Appendix to this chapter. Indirect evidence that it was normative in these groups to hold and express liberal views, and that liberalism served as a standard of evaluation, is given in the next section.

TABLE 4.4
RANK, CENTRALITY, AND INFLUENCE IN THE
DISCUSSION GROUPS

High Centrality

INFLUENCE

Rank	High-Med.	Low	Total
High	16	4	20
Med-Low	9	2	11
Total	25	6	31

$h = -.06$

Medium Centrality

INFLUENCE

Rank	High-Med.	Low	Total
High	12	7	19
Med-Low	4	16	20
Total	16	23	39

$h = .74$

Low Centrality

INFLUENCE

Rank	High-Med.	Low	Total
Hi-Med	1	8	9
Low	2	20	22
Total	3	28	31

$h = .11$

The findings are presented first and then discussed. As may be seen in Tables 4.5, 4.6, and 4.7, conformity is associated with both centrality (Proposition 4) and influence (Proposition 9), and when introduced into the relationship between them, affects the distribution of influence within each degree of centrality. The numbers are necessarily small, but the relationship is quite regular. (Conformity in these tables is final conformity, i.e., conformity at the end of the six-week period.)

TABLE 4.5
CENTRALITY AND FINAL CONFORMITY IN THE
DISCUSSION GROUPS

| | Final Conformity | | | |
Centrality	High	Low	Total	N
High	61	39	100%	31
Medium	69	31	100%	35
Low	10	90	100%	29
Total	49	51	100%	95 *

$h = .58$

* Six campers had left the encampment, permanently or just for the day, at the time the final questionnaires were being filled out.

TABLE 4.6
FINAL CONFORMITY AND INFLUENCE IN THE
DISCUSSION GROUPS

| Final Conformity | Influence | | | | |
	High	Medium	Low	Total	N
High	49	17	34	100%	47
Low	21	4	75	100%	48
Total	35	10	55	100%	95 *

$h = .62$

*See note to Table 4.5.

High conformity clearly appears to facilitate the exercise of influence, as we would expect it to, for the reason given when Proposition 9 was discussed in Chapter 3: The more a member's sentiments and ideas correspond to those that are normative in the group (conformity), the more likely it is that his behaviors will be in accord with these group norms (influence through reinforcement). Nevertheless, influence results from actually expressing appropriate ideas, not from merely holding them, and the effects of conformity are clear only when the members' degrees of centrality are held constant.

TABLE 4.7
CENTRALITY, FINAL CONFORMITY, AND INFLUENCE
IN THE DISCUSSION GROUPS

		Influence			
	Final	High-Med.	Low	Total	N
Centrality	Conformity				
High	High	89	11	100%	19
	Low	67	33	100%	12
Medium	High	54	46	100%	24
	Low	18	82	100%	11
Low	High	25	75	100%	4
	Low	8	92	100%	25

The figures in Table 4.5, however, to turn back to them, are not entirely in accord with what one would expect to observe on the basis of Proposition 4. The proportion relatively high on final conformity in these groups was in fact somewhat larger among those medium on centrality (69 percent) than among those high on centrality (61 percent), whereas the theory would lead us to expect the opposite. This reversal is not true for *initial* conformity: 73 percent of those high on centrality at the end of the program were, when it began, among the more conforming members of their groups, whereas for those medium on centrality at the end the comparable figure is 61 percent. The implication here—that those high on centrality were relatively *less* influenced by the group than those medium on centrality, so much so that they became relatively less conforming over the course of the program—is supported by change data. These show that among those initially below the liberalism of the encampment as a whole, those who averaged the most positive change on the dimension of liberalism were at the end far more often among those medium on centrality than among those high on centrality.

It seems possible to interpret these results in two ways, but first some comments on the main proposition are in order. The reasoning behind the centrality-conformity proposition states that centrality tends to result in conformity in virtue of the actions one *receives* from other members. Any person who, while interacting, initiates action is by definition simultaneously receiving responses from others (in the form of grunts, gestures, etc.). But such ongoing sanctions presumably affect a participant's sentiments and ideas somewhat less than do the sanctions that come in the form of main actions specifically initiated toward him (acts received). It is probably true that for any participant in an interaction system there *tends* to be a rough equivalence between his proportion of the total acts initiated in the group and his proportion of the total acts received, as some work by Bales cited in the Appendix to Chapter 2 shows. But it is only a tendency, and in most groups, it seems reasonable to assume, some members initiate acts out of proportion to those they receive (overparticipators) and some receive acts out of proportion to those they initiate (underparticipators). Consequently, we should probably add a qualification to Proposition 4, making it read as follows: The greater a member's centrality, the greater his conformity, if his centrality relative to other members is the same as his acts-received relative to other members.

One interpretation of the result reported in Table 4.5 is in terms of the validity of the indicator of centrality being used here. For it seems quite possible that this indicator reflects rather more than is desirable the two kinds of out-of-line participants mentioned above, the overparticipators and the underparticipators. The answers providing the information for classifying participants with respect to centrality were secured by questions that specifically asked about over- and underparticipation (see the Appendix to this chapter). Whereas those mentioned as underparticipators have probably not been misclassified to any great extent, the same cannot be said of those mentioned as overparticipators. Some people are undoubtedly classified as high on centrality who merely talked too much relative to what the others considered to be a reasonable amount for them to talk. These procedural deviants, moreover, as their very overparticipation implies, were probably the members who, relative to the others, were least sensitive to sanctions, and consequently would probably have had to receive relatively more acts than others for their degree of conformity to have kept up with the increasingly liberal group standards. Insofar as such a misclassification has occurred, then, findings of the sort reported in Table 4.5 would result.

The other interpretation assumes the members have been classified correctly and introduces the notion that the very influence which the most central members in each group exercised is responsible for the decrease in their relative conformity. There seems to be no reason to doubt that, overparticipators or not, the most central members were the most influential (Table 4.2). What might have happened, at least to some extent, is that they were too successful as influentials. Some among them, namely, those whose acts-initiated were out of proportion to their acts-received, may have contributed to moving group opinion past their own level of conformity. In effect, this interpretation suggests that those who were initially opinion-followers in the groups "outgrew" some who were initially opinion-leaders.

It may not be common for an opinion-leader so to influence his followers that they outgrow him, in the sense of becoming more conforming to the standards he supports than he himself is, but it probably is not rare either. And when it does occur, it may have an important function. For as will be discussed in the next chapter, the theory can be interpreted as describing a process which contains within it a "differentiating tendency," that is, a tendency for a steadily widening gap to develop between the extremes on a group's distributions of rank, influence, and the intervening properties. Insofar as the exercise of influence tends to erase differences in conformity between the extremes, this differentiating tendency is clearly checked. The point is only noted here in passing, its development being reserved for the next chapter.

In summary, the data presented in this section indicate that a fairly definite structuring of influence evolved within the discussion groups over the course of the six weeks. Moreover, the structures were of the sort the theory suggests should have evolved: The higher-ranking members were also the more influential, and this was so in virtue of their greater centrality; and at each level of centrality, the more conforming participants were also the more influential. In the next section, some of the developments during the six weeks that led to this structuring of influence are examined.

Developmental Sequences

At the very beginning, campers differed among themselves on none of the properties, since the groups as such hardly existed. There were, however, certain initial differences among them that shaped the evolution of the interaction systems of the groups, and two of these differences are particularly important here. Viewing them in terms of the theory will allow us to make and check some inferences about the probable sequences and mechanisms involved in the development of the structures just described.

The Mechanism of the Shifting Majority. Of the many substantive areas in the normative consensus of the encampment, we focus here on one, the area of liberalism. The holding and expressing of liberal opinions and sentiments apparently became normative early in the six-week period, and liberalism appears to have been the principal standard used by participants in most interaction contexts to evaluate one another's actions. For the moment we shall have to assume that this happened, although some evidence is presented in passing which suggests that liberalism was a standard of appraisal within the discussion groups.

Perhaps the most important feature of the consensus on liberalism was the presence of a condition which permitted the operation of what I shall call here "the mechanism of the shifting majority." It is sometimes assumed by researchers that the concept of a group norm or standard reduces operationally to some sort of an average over the participants. Many theorists, on the other hand, among whom Durkheim is perhaps the most prominent, contend that the notion of an average is an incorrect rendering of the concept, that a group is in some sense more than the simple sum of its members, and in particular that group standards as reflected in the views of the average member appear to be a good deal weaker than they in fact are.

There is an important point to Durkheim's argument, as is shown in the simple diagram below of a three-man group whose consensus consists of three norms. The "average member" of this group is committed to only two of the three sentiments (indicated by the "x's"), but if the majority rule is applied, as it usually is in the measurement of consensus, the group as a whole is committed to all three.

		Member's Degree of
Member	Norms	Conformity
	1 2 3	
A	x x	.67
B	x x	.67
C	x x	.67

Included in
Group Consensus: x x x

The data on liberalism at the encampment conform approximately to this "model." When they arrived most participants were, as was said, fairly liberal, but they differed not only in degree but also in the particular matters on which they held highly liberal views. There was always, or almost always, a majority supporting the liberal position on any particular issue, but from issue to issue the composition of the liberal majority changed, the particular campers who composed it varying somewhat with each issue. A particular participant was in the majority, then, more or less often depending on how liberal he was or became, but each was also in the minority at one time or another and hence subject to majority pressures.

Specifically, of the 30 items on the liberalism battery, 26 were initially endorsed by a majority of the participants, whereas the median of the participants' scores was only 22. On issues of the sort that would come up frequently in the succeeding six weeks, therefore, the encampment as a whole would take the liberal position approximately nine times out of ten on the average, whereas the average participant would take that position no more than about three times out of four. The degree of commitment to liberalism on the part of both the encampment as a whole and its average member increased over the six weeks, the median participant having a score of about 26 by the end and a majority of participants endorsing 29 of the 30 items at the end (the slight difference suggesting that the level of conformity increased also). Nevertheless, throughout the six weeks, the encampment was clearly more liberal than its average member, in the quite specific sense that the average member's degree of commitment to liberalism was measurably less than the degree of commitment of the encampment as a whole.

Conformity-Rank.　What is true of the encampment is approximately true as well of each of the nine discussion groups. They differed to some extent, both initially and finally, in the liberalism of their median member, but at both times each discussion group was more liberal than its average member. There thus existed initially in each certain latent pressures toward change, pressures that would be felt more strongly by some members than by others but by every member at one point or another.

The pressures presumably made themselves felt in the form
of sanctions, that is, in the form of the responses the campers
made to one another's expressions of opinion during the discussions. On the average, if a member expressed a liberal
sentiment, the chances were about nine out of ten that a
majority of others would approve of the sentiment expressed
and thus (assuming for the moment no relation between initial
conformity and centrality) that the overt response(s) to his
expressed view would be positive. In other words, given the
initial distribution of opinion, the expression of a liberal sentiment usually amounted to exercising influence by reinforcing
shared ideas and to being positively sanctioned for doing so.

Proposition 14, linking the exercise of influence directly to
rank, on the grounds that a member who visibly complies with
the group's norms both reinforces the norms (influence) and
receives positive sanctions from others (rank), is the most
relevant here. We lack direct information on early differences
in influence among the members, but can approach the matter
indirectly. One step back in the sequence, so to speak, is
Proposition 9, which links conformity to the exercise of influence on the assumption, stated earlier, that the more a
member's normative commitments correspond to group norms,
the more likely it is that his behavior will be in accord with
the group norms. It follows from these two propositions that
the greater a member's relative conformity at time one, the
higher his relative rank at time two.

Since we know the campers' initial liberalism scores, we can
see whether this derivation applies to the encampment. Table
4.8 relates conformity at the beginning of the program to
rank at the end. As it shows, those who were initially the more
conforming, compared with those who were initially less conforming, were almost twice as likely to become high-ranking
members of their group by the end, and less than half as
likely to become low-ranking members.

These data bear on the assumption, mentioned earlier, that

liberalism served from the start as the standard of appraisal in the discussion groups. At the least, they are consistent with the hypothesis that it did.

TABLE 4.8
INITIAL CONFORMITY AND RANK IN THE
DISCUSSION GROUPS

Initial Conformity	High	Rank Medium	Low	Total	N
High	54	29	17	100%	48
Low	29	25	46	100%	41
Total	43	27	30	100%	89*

$h = .49$

* Twelve campers did not arrive in time to fill out the first questionnaire.

Predispositions, Centrality, and Ranking. At the very start, before interaction began, differences in centrality were of course nonexistent, but there were nevertheless differences among participants in a highly relevant predisposition. The widespread institutionalization of discussion groups makes it probable that each participant arrived at the encampment, not only with a fairly well internalized "discussion role," but also with a fairly definite disposition, arising out of his past experience and perhaps certain basic personality characteristics, to play a more or a less active role in discussions. Presumably, since the situation in the groups at the start was relatively unstructured, at least with respect to how campers stood relative to one another, these predispositions tended to be acted out and thus to generate corresponding differences in centrality.

In the present case, predispositions of this sort could have two principal effects on the development of a group's interaction system, depending upon the relationship between predispositions and initial conformity. If those inclined to be active participants in discussions also conformed more initially, the predispositions would have directly facilitated the development of the interaction system, since centrality would have been distributed from the start approximately as it was to be distributed at the end. If the actively inclined were initially the less conforming, however, the predispositions would have directly hindered the development of the observed structures, since it would have been necessary to effect a redistribution of centrality. The actively disposed nonconformists would have had to become more liberal or to participate in discussions less (and less than they were used to doing), and the passively disposed conformists would have had to take a more active part (and more active than they were used to taking).

As it happened, most participants arrived at the encampment with characteristics suited to the needs of the program. Those predisposed to take an active part in discussions were two to three times as likely as the others to be among the initially more conforming members of their discussion group (which again supports the assumption that liberalism early became operative as a standard of appraisal). Nevertheless, there remained about a third of the participants (27 out of the 83 for whom we have the necessary information) who, at the start, combined traits that were incompatible from the point of view of a group's interaction system. Interpreting the rank-centrality hypothesis as stating a sequential relation between the two properties—so that variations in rank at time one lead to similar variations in centrality at time two—we should find that the ranking processes in the discussion groups effected some changes among these 27.

And they seem to have done so, especially among the 14 more visible deviants who began with the "incompatible" combination of an inclination to be active and a low degree of conformity.[3] Of these, 7 became active conformers by the end (high or medium on centrality, high on conformity), 5 became passive nonconformers (low on centrality and conformity), 2 remained as they were (high or medium on centrality, low on conformity), and none acquired the contrary set of incom-

---

[3] The indicator of the predisposition to be active or passive in discussions is described in the Appendix to this chapter.

patible traits. Of the 13 who began with the opposite pair of "incompatible" traits—an inclination to be passive in discussions but high on initial conformity—6 became active conformers, 1 a passive nonconformer, 3 remained as they were, and 3 developed the opposite set of incompatible traits. Out of the 27 potentially disturbing participants, then, 19, or 70 percent, were "brought into line" by, presumably, the groups' sanctioning processes.

That it was probably the sanctioning processes which brought them into line is indicated by the distribution of high rank among these participants at the end. For example, of the 14 with the incompatible combination of an active inclination and low initial conformity, 8 were accorded high rank at the end and 6 were not; of the 8 who were, the majority (6) in fact took an active part but changed their views, becoming by the end more liberal than the average member of their group; of the 6 who were not accorded high rank, the majority (4) remained among the less liberal members of their group but lowered their characteristic rate of participation, becoming by the end relatively inactive.

The numbers are minuscule but the patterns are consistent, and it seems reasonable to infer from these data that they point to one of the ways in which an interaction system acts on its psychological environment and prevents potentially disruptive effects from making themselves felt. This specific argument, however, as well as the general formulation given earlier, assumes that ranking has definite kinds of motivational effects, and we turn now to some data relevant to that assumption.

The Sense of Belonging. By the end of the encampment those who were accorded relatively high rank in their discussion groups were usually relatively high on centrality also, and those accorded low rank, low on centrality. These "ranks" were specific to each group, even perhaps to the particular members of each group; they certainly were not institutionalized features of clearly differentiated roles. The rank-centrality relationship at the end of the program thus probably reflected fairly directly the effects of the ranking process on participation—that is, the tendency for approvals to have encouraged participation and for disapprovals to have discouraged it—rather than normatively required differences in participation associated with rank-differences. What seems to have happened is that the same process which generated the differences in rank, the sanctioning process, generated parallel differences in motivation at the same time, and these motivational differences gave rise in turn to parallel differences in actual participation.

In order to gauge whether differences in motivation were related to differences in rank on the one hand and in centrality on the other, it is necessary to assume that the less a member felt a part of his group, the less he was motivated to participate actively, or at least, the more hesitant he was about doing so. That is, it is necessary to assume a close relationship between differences in sense of belonging and differences in motivation to participate. (The indicator of sense of belonging is described in the Appendix to this chapter.)

First we consider the relationships at the end of the program between rank and sense of belonging, and between this feeling and centrality (Tables 4.9 and 4.10).

TABLE 4.9
RANK AND SENSE OF BELONGING IN THE
DISCUSSION GROUPS

Rank	Sense of Belonging		Total	N
	High	Low		
High	85	15	100%	40
Medium	71	29	100%	24
Low	33	67	100%	30
Total	65	35	100%	94 *

$h = .69$

* Six campers were not present to fill out the final questionnaire and one skipped the page the felt-belonging question was on.

With respect to the first, it seems clear that members with a higher ratio of positive to negative sanctions, that is, with a high or medium rank, were much less likely than those with a low rank to feel they did not really belong. And with respect to the second, it seems clear that those who felt they did not belong, compared with those who did, were far less likely to be high or medium on centrality.

TABLE 4.10
SENSE OF BELONGING AND CENTRALITY IN THE DISCUSSION GROUPS

Sense of Belonging	High	Centrality Medium	Low	Total	N
High	43	44	13	100%	61
Low	12	24	64	100%	33
Total	32	37	31	100%	94 *

$h = .73$

* See note to Table 4.9.

As was stated earlier, however, the motivational effects of the ranking process are only a part of the reason for the rank-centrality relationship. They affect only the acts-initiated component, so to speak, and not also the acts received. The sense of belonging should therefore condition the rank-centrality relation, which it does (Table 4.11), but it should not be a necessary link between them, which it is not. Those with high or medium rank are more likely to be central if they feel they belong than if they do not, but they are more likely to be central than those with low rank whether or not they feel they belong.

It seems likely that in these groups it was mainly differences in the negative sanctioning, in conjunction with different predispositions to participate, that generated the actual participation differences. It was less a case of an unequal distribution of approvals encouraging some to participate more than others than a case of an unequal distribution of disapprovals discouraging some from participating as much as others. One indication of this occurs when sense of belonging is viewed in relation to both initial predispositions (initial centrality) and

TABLE 4.11
RANK, SENSE OF BELONGING, AND CENTRALITY
IN THE DISCUSSION GROUPS

Rank	Sense of Belonging	High	Centrality Medium	Low	Total	N
High	High	50	47	3	100%	34
	Low	33	50	17	100%	6
Medium	High	47	29	24	100%	17
	Low	25	38	38	101%	8
Low	High	10	60	30	100%	10
	Low	0	11	89	100%	19

final levels of participation (final centrality). As Table 4.12
clearly suggests, by developing in some the feeling that they
did not really belong, the sanctioning process depressed their
actual levels of participation considerably.

TABLE 4.12
INITIAL DISPOSITION TO PARTICIPATE, SENSE OF
BELONGING, AND CENTRALITY IN THE DISCUSSION
GROUPS

Initially Disposed to Participate:	Sense of Belonging at End:	High	Centrality at End Medium	Low	Total	N*
Actively	High	50	42	8	100%	38
	Low	25	25	50	101%	8
Passively	High	18	65	18	101%	17
	Low	11	21	68	100%	19

* Altogether, 17 campers failed to fill out one or both questionnaires,
and there was one NA on each of the disposition and sense-of-belonging
questions.

As a result of the negative sanctioning, each group contained
on the average two or three members who were being alienated,
both in the sense of being pushed out of the group and in the
sense of withdrawing from it. The effects of this alienative process are very clear in Table 4.11. Of those both accorded low rank
by others and feeling they did not really belong, 9 out of 10

(compared with 1 out of 5 of the others) were low on centrality. And as by now would be expected, those made to feel they did not belong were the less conforming: Among those who were more conforming at both times, 86 percent felt they were really a part of their discussion group; among those who were more conforming either at the beginning or at the end, the figure was 64 percent; but among those who were less conforming at both times, only 36 percent came to feel they really belonged.

Summary. Initially, then, each group was more liberal than most of its members, and those who were the more conforming were also likely to be predisposed to take an active rather than a passive part in discussions. Relative centrality and relative conformity were therefore associated from the start, and in consequence so presumably were relative centrality and relative influence. The frequent expression of liberal views that resulted (a) reinforced their salience in the group's developing consensus and made it increasingly liberal, (b) secured for the speakers the approval of their peers, thus in time making relative rank parallel with the other three properties, and (c), insofar as the approvals were visibly expressed, indicated clearly to all that on most matters the group as a whole was highly liberal.

Not every expressed opinion was liberal, of course. Initially some members were actively inclined but less liberal than most. And in any case, those who were passively inclined were only inclined that way relatively; they still spoke up occasionally. When expressed, though, nonliberal views met with indifference or disapproval by the majority, at least most of the time, and the members who continued to express them became in time disapproved of. They in turn developed the feeling that they were not really a part of the group, a feeling that had the effect of depressing still further their usually already low level of participation. Nonconforming to begin with, and for the most part predisposed to play a passive role in discussions, they exercised little influence, were relatively often negatively sanctioned, and became progressively less motivated to take an active part in discussions. By the end of the six weeks, they were clearly distinguishable from the majority of the members in a group, being uniformly low on all key properties of the status of group member.

In the larger study the effects of the program as a whole are shown to result in large part from the operation of the nine discussion groups, which thus appear to have functioned as relatively effective influence structures within the over-all organization. A similar analysis of the ten dormitory groups, however, shows that they were not effective as influence structures, and the next section examines why this was so. Before concluding this discussion, however, the introduction here of motivational variables deserves to be commented upon.

In Chapter 2, it was said that psychological factors would be considered not as variables in the theory, but as external factors affecting the analytic relationships of a narrowly circumscribed interaction system. The material in this section illustrates the introduction of such factors into an analysis, but it can also be used to show why they are not fully incorporated into the theory.

Even the crude indicators that had to be used here of motivational states serve to indicate the considerable dependence of differences in centrality on differences in motivation. There is no reason to doubt the usefulness of the general orientation that such states are causally relevant to a group's interaction system. Moreover, in some groups (such as the discussion groups) it happens that the ranking process of their interaction system has an effect on the members' motivations to participate that is greater than the effects of the host of other external factors affecting motivation. It is one thing, however, to say that variations in motivation may be relevant to centrality, or to say that sometimes a group's ranking process is the principal determinant of these variations; and it is another to state as a principal proposition of a theory that a group's ranking process (or any other group process) is gener-

ally the principal determinant of the members' motivation to participate. An examination of why the ranking process was so effective in the case of the discussion groups suggests why it is not useful to assume that generally it is so effective.

What is striking about the situation of the discussion groups is that their psychological environment was unusually suited to their requirements. First, for almost all the participants, virtually all other membership statuses and associated roles were latent during the full six-week period. Second, almost every other membership status acquired within the encampment carried with it the same basic normative obligation—to hold and express liberal views—and placed its occupant in a similar situation—subject to sanctions in support of this obligation. Third, most individuals displayed from the start one or the other of the basic combinations of subjective states required for a discussion group's interaction system to operate effectively.

Few groups, it seems safe to assume, operate in a psychological environment so consistent with their motivational requirements. Most have to contend instead with innumerable sources of what, from their point of view, are random variations in their members' motivation to participate. In general, a group's sanctioning process tends to structure motivations so that they parallel group-accorded ranks; but in most groups this is no more than a tendency. Many other factors, well outside the ordinary scope of control of small-group processes, affect members' motivations, and it is seldom true in consequence that a group's ranking process is the principal determinant of these motivations.

Motivation to participate, is, then, causally relevant to influence through its relevance for centrality. But it remains outside the variables of an interaction system, since it would seem so often to vary independently of them.

Forms of Interaction and Structures of Influence

The influence structures which evolved within the discussion groups and which by the end of the program took the form described earlier, appear to have been relatively effective at the individual level. They seem to have generated in the initially less liberal campers the kinds of changes the program intended to produce and to have prevented among the initially more liberal campers the kinds of changes the program did not intend to produce. At least there is a very strong relationship between the part each camper played in his discussion group's interaction system and the program's measured impact on him.

No such relationship obtains, however, between a camper's part in his *dormitory* group and the program's over-all effect on him. This is somewhat surprising in view of the fact that both kinds of groups had almost identical personnel during an identical period of time; the initial conditions within both were thus about the same; and the interaction systems of all nineteen groups evolved in virtually identical psychological, social, and physical environments. The larger study goes into this matter more fully than it is possible to do here. One line of argument from the fuller analysis is particularly pertinent to the present essay, though, and is presented below, since it bears on the importance given here to a group's form of interaction, that is, to its frequency of set events.

Dormitory groups and discussion groups differ "culturally," of course. The accepted norms pertaining to social relations among roommates are different from those pertaining to relations among discussion-group members, and the recognized responsibilities of staff members as dormitory leaders are different from their responsibilities as discussion-group leaders. In particular, in the sort of informal discussions or bull sessions that regularly occurred in the dormitory groups in the late evening, there are not usually any strong norms to the effect that every member should participate in the main discussion or that each should refrain from talking while another is speaking.

Nor were the staff members of a dormitory group responsible for "running" the discussions that took place.

Partly as a result of these cultural or normative differences and partly as a result of others of a similar sort—the defined purposes of the two groups were quite different, for example —their interaction systems took quite different forms. As has been said, interaction in a discussion group almost always occurred in the form of set events: The groups met at regularly scheduled times for stated intervals of time and usually with everyone present; there was in each a single common activity and a single center of activity (the discussion leader); and the interaction that occurred engaged most of the participants most of the time. In the dormitory groups, in contrast, interaction frequently occurred not only in the form of set events but also in the form of pair or triadic events. (I shall speak of these, loosely, as "subgroup events," even though subgroups proper, that is, of the sort discussed in Chapter 2, appear to have developed in only one or two of the dormitory units.) Many conversations took place over the course of the day among roommates who happened to be together in the dormitory room at the same time. And even when, as in the morning briefly and in the late evening for a fairly long period, all or most members were present, several conversations could and presumably did occur simultaneously.

This difference in their form of interaction gave rise to a parallel difference in the influence structures of the two kinds of groups. There was a certain degree of similarity: In the dormitory groups as in the discussion groups, rank, sense of belonging, centrality, conformity, and influence were all positively associated at the end of the encampment (although the relationships were not so strong in the former as in the latter). But whereas influence was always exercised in the discussion groups in the context of set events, and hence was primarily influence on group opinion, in the dormitory units it was exercised as often as not in the context of subgroup events, and in such instances did not affect group opinion, at least not directly, so much as it affected the opinions of one or another particular member.

The centrality that was associated with influence in the dormitory groups was thus composed, so to speak, of two different kinds of centrality. There was centrality in set events, or what I shall call, for present purposes, group-level centrality; and there was centrality in subgroup events, or what I shall call interpersonal centrality. The two of course could have coincided—a member who participated a great deal in the late evening discussions, or other set events, could also have participated a great deal in the various subgroup events that occurred over the course of a day in a dormitory—but they need not have done so. Similarly, a member could have been highly influential at the group level, that is, in the sense of directly affecting group opinion, without having been influential at the interpersonal level, that is, in the sense of directly influencing particular others' opinions in subgroup contexts; and vice versa.

Owing to our measurement of influence, we can only know for each group who exercised more or less influence; we have no way of distinguishing between those whose influence was primarily on group opinion (social influence) and those whose influence was primarily on individuals' opinions (personal influence). We can, however, distinguish crudely between relative centrality in set events, that is, in participation at the group level, and relative centrality in subgroup events, that is, in participation at the interpersonal level.[4] (See the Appendix to this chapter for the indicators used.) If the contrast between the two groups is rightly drawn, and if the analysis based upon the contrast is a reasonable one, we should observe two things: First, the relationship between centrality in set events and influence should be much stronger in the discussion groups than in the dormitory groups. Second, the relationship between centrality in interpersonal events and influence should be much stronger in the dormitory groups than in the discussion groups.

[4] In preceding sections, only what is here referred to as group-level centrality was discussed.

As for the first hypothesis, Table 4.13 contains the relevant information. (Descriptions of the indicators of the concepts are given in the Appendix to the chapter.) Quite clearly, the data are consistent with the first hypothesis.

TABLE 4.13
GROUP-LEVEL CENTRALITY AND INFLUENCE IN THE
DISCUSSION GROUPS AND IN THE DORMITORY
GROUPS

DISCUSSION GROUPS

Group-Level Centrality	High	Influence Medium	Low	Total	N
High	77	3	19	99%	31
Medium	26	15	59	100%	39
Low	0	10	90	100%	31

$h = .82$

DORMITORY GROUPS

Group-Level Centrality	High	Influence Medium	Low	Total	N
High	61	9	30	100%	54
Medium	40	28	32	100%	25
Low	29	29	43	101%	14

$h = .26$

As for the second hypothesis, that the relationship between interpersonal participation and influence was stronger in the dormitory groups than in the discussion groups, Table 4.14 contains the necessary information. Again, the hypothesis is supported by the data available.

If virtually all interaction in the discussion groups is in the form of set events, though, then in these groups only group-level centrality should be related to influence. Whatever influence interpersonal centrality appears to carry should be merely a reflection of a positive relationship between such centrality and group-level centrality. In the dormitory groups, on the other hand, where interaction takes both forms and a member's centrality in the full network of his dormitory's interaction se-

TABLE 4.14
INTERPERSONAL CENTRALITY AND INFLUENCE IN
THE DISCUSSION GROUPS AND IN THE
DORMITORY GROUPS

DISCUSSION GROUPS

Interpersonal Centrality	High	Influence Medium	Low	Total	N
High	39	13	48	100%	46
Medium	32	7	61	100%	44
Low	18	9	73	100%	11

$h = .26$

DORMITORY GROUPS

Interpersonal Centrality	High	Influence Medium	Low	Total	N
High	66	15	20	101%	41
Medium	42	13	44	99%	45
Low	27	27	47	101%	15

$h = .42$

quences is thus a combination of his group-level centrality and his interpersonal centrality, both modes of participation should carry influence. Tables 4.15 and 4.16 present the data.

TABLE 4.15
GROUP-LEVEL CENTRALITY, INTERPERSONAL
CENTRALITY, AND INFLUENCE IN THE
DISCUSSION GROUPS

	Centrality		Influence		
Group Level	Interpersonal	High	Med-Low	Total	
High	High	81	19	100%	
	Med-low	71	29	100%	
Medium	High	18	82	100%	
	Med-low	35	65	100%	
Low	High	0	100	100%	
	Med-low	0	100	100%	

As is evident, there is little regularity in the relationship between interpersonal centrality and influence in the discussion groups when group-level centrality is held constant. On the other hand, in the dormitory groups, both kinds of centrality are independently related to influence; moreover, as would be expected from Tables 4.13 and 4.14, interpersonal centrality is more of a determinant of influence in these groups than is group-level centrality.

TABLE 4.16
GROUP-LEVEL CENTRALITY, INTERPERSONAL
CENTRALITY, AND INFLUENCE IN THE
DORMITORY GROUPS

Centrality		Influence		
Interpersonal	Group Level	High	Med-Low	Total
High	High	76	24	100%
	Med-low	53	47	100%
Medium	High	48	52	100%
	Med-low	33	67	100%
Low	High	37	63	100%
	Med-low	0	100	100%

The general picture that emerges from this comparison is of groups differing more or less markedly in their patterns of interaction. At one extreme are groups like the discussion groups, where virtually all interaction is in the form of set events. At the other extreme are groups like those in most experiments using communications net, where all interaction is in the form of pair events. No groups of the latter sort existed at the encampment, but the dormitory units resembled this type.

Paralleling the patterns of interaction are certain patterns of influence. In centrally organized interaction systems, influence is exercised not so much on individuals as on group opinion (social influence). In dyadically organized systems, influence is exercised directly by one person on another (personal influence). As a result of the first, individual opinions may change, and as a result of the second, group opinions may change, but the sequence of effects is reversed in the two cases. Both modes of exercising influence probably occur to some extent in all groups, but in different proportions, depending upon the characteristic form of interaction. In the groups under study, social influence dominated the influence process in the discussion groups to the virtual exclusion of interpersonal influence; interpersonal influence, on the other hand, was much more important in the dormitories.

Of course, the fact that influence in the dormitories was often interpersonal rather than social does not by itself explain why the dormitories appear to have generated so little change in a liberal direction. There remains, then, another step to the analysis. Having seen that the mode of exercising influence was a function of the form of interaction, we must now see whether the mode of exercising influence can in turn account for the reported differences in the effectiveness of the two kinds of groups.

It is possible in principle, of course, that influence exercised through interpersonal relations generated the program's measured effects, but it seems unlikely that it did. For interpersonal influence appears to be an inherently weaker kind of pressure than group-level influence, at least as far as inducing conformity to group standards is concerned. This is so, first, because the impact of opinions counter to one's own is ordinarily less in interpersonal contexts than in group contexts and, second, because the kinds of people likely to become interpersonally influential tend to reflect not the group-held standards so much as the standards held by the average member.

As for the first, whenever during group-level discussions in any of these groups someone voiced a nonliberal view, those most likely to respond explicitly, and to address themselves to the speaker, were the more central members, who were more likely than any of the others to hold highly liberal views on the matter. Hence, the explicit response to a nonliberal view was likely to be negative. It was also likely that a majority of the others held liberal views on the matter, in which case they would probably have indicated their support for the central members' views in some way (nodding of head, verbal approval, etc.). Hence, diffuse pressures as well were likely to be exerted. Insofar as a camper who found himself disagreeing with a leading member of a group cared at all about his peers' opinions of him (that is, about his rank in the group), he could not but be affected by visible expressions of *group* opinion. Social influence, then, by working through opinion leadership in set events and acting primarily on group opinion, derives its force to affect an individual member's opinions from the fact that it brings visibly into play both the mechanism of the shifting majority and the group's ranking process.

Virtually all of this is absent in interpersonal influence. The higher-ranking members of a group may be, perhaps usually are, the interpersonally influential members. Nevertheless, at the point that influence is exercised the group's ranking process only structures the situation—a higher-ranking member is simply more likely to exert direct personal influence on a lower-ranking member than *vice versa*. The process itself does not operate in the course of the interaction sequence through which the influence is exercised (or, if it is assumed to be always operative, it operates in an attenuated form). For unless the group is actually present, an ordinary member is uncertain whether the leading member's views reflect group sentiments, and even if he feels they may, no group evaluations of him come immediately into play in support of the leading member's sanctions.

This same argument bears on the question of the kinds of people likely to become interpersonally influential. The approvals given in interpersonal contexts of interaction, where group opinion is necessarily less visible, are likely to reflect not conformity with group standards so much as "conformity" with the standards that the two or three participants in any "subgroup" happen to hold. The relation between conformity and centrality, therefore, is likely to be a good deal less in groups where interpersonal interaction bulks large than in groups where such interaction is a negligible proportion of the total. And in consequence, the relation between conformity and interpersonal influence is also likely to be relatively weak. Or, to put it another way, the interpersonally influential member will tend to have about the same level of conformity as the average member (that is, to "conform" to the average), in contrast to the influential exercising influence at the group level, who, owing to the effects of the ranking process, in conjunction with the mechanism of the shifting majority, tends to conform to operative group standards more than the average member does.

And in fact, if we examine the data from the dormitory groups bearing on this point, we find that those who "specialized" in interpersonal influence were *not* among the notably liberal members (Table 4.17). Those whose influence derived primarily from their centrality in interpersonal relations were as often as not among the less conforming members of their dormitories, while those whose influence derived from their centrality at both levels were only somewhat more likely than not to be among the more conforming. Only those whose influence derived primarily from their high participation at the group-level—that is, in set events—were much more often than not among the more conforming members of their dormitory unit.

TABLE 4.17
GROUP-LEVEL CENTRALITY, INTERPERSONAL
CENTRALITY, AND FINAL CONFORMITY AMONG
THOSE RELATIVELY INFLUENTIAL IN THEIR
DORMITORY GROUPS

Channel for Exercising Influence		*Conformity at End*			
Group-Level Centrality	Interpersonal Centrality	High	Low	Totals	N*
High	Not High	86	14	100%	14
High	High	58	42	100%	19
Low	High	25	75	100%	8

* Of the 50 who were relatively influential in their dormitory groups, 6 were central by neither criterion and are ignored here, and 3 failed to fill out the final questionnaire.

In summary, then, the dormitory groups were less effective than the discussion groups in generating the kinds of effects that made the program successful, because, first, interaction frequently occurred in the context of interpersonal relations; second, influence in consequence was also often exercised in such contexts; and third, neither the process of exercising influence in interpersonal relations nor the kinds of people influential in these contexts are likely to exert as much pressure in support of groups standards as is exerted in the course of interaction in set events.

Summary

Two uses of the body of concepts and propositions developed in Chapters 2 and 3 were exemplified in this chapter. In the first part, the theory was interpreted as implying a concept of leadership, and material from Whyte's classic account of cornerboy leaders was used to illustrate the kind of description and mode of analysis the conception involves. In addition, two issues occasionally encountered in leadership studies were discussed, the question of conformity *versus* innovation and the question of popularity as a characteristic of leaders.

In the second part of the chapter, the theory was interpreted as implying developmental relationships among the properties, and material from a study of a training program was used to illustrate this kind of application. The structuring of influence at the end of the program in nine of its working units was described in terms of the theory, the factual relations that emerged being what we would expect them to be on the basis of the theory. Some of the processes which helped produce the observed structuring were also described. In the third section the effect of a group's form of interaction on its influence structure was illustrated by a comparison between two different kinds of groups in the program.

The next chapter discusses one more use of the theory, namely, depicting a process basic to the interaction system of small groups.

Appendix to Chapter 4

Concepts and Indicators in the Training Program Study

The indicators of the following concepts are described here in the order given: Liberalism; the properties of discussion-group members (rank, group-level centrality, interpersonal centrality, influence, conformity, and sense of belonging); the predisposition to take an active or a passive part in discussions; and the properties of dormitory-group members (group-level centrality, interpersonal centrality, influence, and conformity).

Liberalism

Campers checked whether they agreed with, disagreed with, or were not sure how they felt about 30 items concerning such matters as civil rights, civil liberties, tolerance of political and religious nonconformity, political action, and so forth. Each item was clearly relevant to the liberal position on social and political matters, and a response was scored as either in line with that position or not in line with it. Scores could thus range in principle from 0 to 30. Individual campers' scores in fact ranged from 12 to 30. The liberalism score of a collective unit—the encampment as a whole or a subgroup—is the number of items to which half or more of the members of the unit gave the liberal response. A detailed account of the selection of the items, together with a complete list of them, is contained in the monograph, *Group Structure and Opinion Change*, cited in full in the text.

Properties of Members of Discussion Groups

Rank

Campers were asked, in the context of questions about their experience in their discussion group, "Thinking over the course of the discussions and of the ideas expressed by various members, with which other members do you usually find yourself agreeing?" For each discussion group separately, the number of mentions (of campers) was totaled and the sum divided by the number of camper-members in order to arrive at a group mean. Those who received more than the group mean were scored as relatively high-ranking, those mentioned at all but who did not receive more than the mean were scored as medium-ranking, and those not mentioned at all, as relatively low-ranking. It was not feasible, given the encampment ethos of democracy and egalitarianism, to ask a direct question about who were the best and worst members of the group. The no-answer rate would probably have been high, and the answers actually received would probably have had a different meaning from the one desired. In using the replies to the question above, I have had to assume that agreement with another's ideas implies a generally high evaluation of the other as a member of the group, but it is not possible to say whether the assumption is warranted. In general, the validity of the indicator is moderate at best; it probably discriminated fairly accurately between the truly medium-ranking and the truly low-ranking members but not very accurately between the high- and the medium-ranking.

Centrality (Group-Level)

In the same battery of questions about their discussion group, campers were asked the following: "During the discussions, which members, if any, tend to talk more than they should, so that some others do not have as much of a chance to give their opinions as they ought to have?" and "Which members, if any, tend to talk less than they should, so that the task of keeping the discussion going falls to others to do?" For each question in each group, the mean number of mentions per camper-member was calculated, and members were scored as above or not above the mean. Those above the mean on the first question are considered to have been relatively high on (group-level) centrality, those above neither mean, to have been medium on centrality, and those above the mean on the second to have been relatively low on centrality. No one was above both means. It would have been better had objective interaction rates been available, but they were not. Discussion-group leaders were asked to turn in, at the end of each week, a rank-ordering of their group's members in terms of participation. In those groups where this was done, the ordering given by the discussion-leader's ratings coincided very closely with the ordering arrived at by the procedure above, suggesting that the indicator probably is fairly valid so far as the acts-initiated component is concerned.

Centrality (Interpersonal)

In the same discussion-group section of the final questionnaire, campers were asked, "Which two or three members do you personally get along with best?" Responses were handled as in the preceding cases: For each group a group-specific mean was computed and members were scored as above the mean or not and, among the latter, as mentioned at all or not mentioned at all, thus again giving three levels, high, medium, and low. It is necessary to assume here that actual interpersonal interaction followed approximately the patterns of interpersonal preferences, which, for the limited purpose at hand, is probably not an unwarranted assumption.

Influence

A rather complex question on influence at the end of the discussion-group section asked campers to estimate whether and to what extent the discussions had affected their opinions in each of several different ways. At the end of this complex question they were asked, "If your opinions have been affected in any way, which particular members have most influenced your opinions?" The replies were handled as in previous cases, a mean for each group being computed and the members being scored relative to their group's mean number of mentions per camper. The face validity of the question is not high; it would have been improved had the question read, Which members have most influenced the group's opinions on the matters discussed? Nevertheless, the question is probably more valid than it seems at first glance: (1) differences in influence measured in this way are highly correlated with differences in conformity, suggesting that it does in fact reflect influence on liberalism; (2) differences in influence are not highly correlated with differences in rank when centrality is held constant, suggesting that the "halo effect" has not contaminated it; and (3) it behaves as it should in the analysis comparing the more personally organized dormitory groups with the more impersonally organized discussion groups.

Conformity

Each group was given a liberalism score on the basis of the number of items, out of the 30 in the battery, to which half or more of its members gave the liberal response. The members were then divided into two groups, those who were more conforming and those who were less conforming, depending upon whether or not their own liberalism score clustered about the group score. In principle, a member could have been highly liberal and nonconforming, that is, he could have been too liberal for his group. In practice, however, this did not occur, and a high (or low) degree of conformity is equivalent to a high (or low) degree of liberalism.

Sense of Belonging

Among the questions asked about the discussion groups was the following, which comes from a battery designed by Michigan researchers for a slightly different purpose (Seashore, 1954, pp. 36-37): "Do you feel you are really a part of your discussion group?", to which respondents could reply, "Really a part," "Included in most ways," "Included in some ways but not in others," and "Don't feel I really belong." All the relationships reported in the text and many others hold up when the fourfold division is used, but because almost two thirds of the respondents checked the first alternative, I have for present purposes collapsed the last three and designated anyone checking one of them as feeling he did not belong.

Predisposition to Take an Active or Passive Part in Discussions

This predisposition was measured by a single question asked on the opening day with reference to discussions of political or social questions among friends or acquaintances at home or at school before coming to the encampment. The question was, "When you and your [pre-encampment] friends discuss political questions, what part do you usually take?" The answer categories were, "I usually just listen," "I listen a lot but once in a while I express my opinion," "I take an equal share in the conversation," and "I usually express my ideas more frequently than others express theirs." Campers checking either of the first two alternatives were scored as relatively passively inclined; those checking either of the latter two, as relatively actively inclined. Responses are highly correlated with responses to several other items bearing on the same matter, and the indicator is probably a rather good one.

Properties of Members in the Dormitory Groups

Centrality (Group-Level)

Group-level centrality in the dormitory groups is indicated by self-estimates in response to a query placed among numerous other questions about the respondent's experiences in his dormitory group. The question was, "How often do you take part in these [late-evening] discussions?" Those who checked "Almost always" are scored as relatively high on (group-level) centrality, those who checked "Usually," as medium on centrality, and those who checked "Occasionally," as relatively low on centrality. No one checked "Almost never." In the light of the definition of the concept, the question is not a particularly good indicator, but it is difficult to assess how inadequate it is.

Centrality (Interpersonal)

A question comparable to the one asked with reference to the respondent's discussion group was asked with reference to his dormitory group. Answers were handled in the same way.

Influence

A question comparable to the one asked with reference to the respondent's experiences in his discussion group was asked with reference to his experiences in his dormitory group. Again, responses were handled in the same way.

Conformity

The procedure used follows exactly the procedure used to classify people as more or less conforming with respect to their discussion group, although here of course the classification was with respect to the liberalism of their dormitory group.

[5]

The Rank-Influence Process

The set of definitions and propositions presented in preceding chapters is used here in a third way, to depict a recurrent process in the interaction systems of small groups which continually distributes and redistributes rank and influence among a group's members. The principal effect of the process is to maintain a high correlation between the two properties, and for this reason its effective operation contributes in a crucial way to the normative structuring of influence and hence to the stability of the structures. The process is also responsible, however, for their instability, since it may produce disturbing effects on the distribution of influence in its own right and is in any case the agency through which other factors transmit their disturbing effects.

The Conjunction of Influence and Rank

In outline, a typical cycle of the process looks as follows. Let us assume that the members of a group differ with respect to the five properties. Each time they come together, the rank differences become salient and guide the interaction; the predictable participation differences emerge, as do their equally predictable effects on conformity, observability, and influence; finally, the influential actions are, usually, actions of the kind that also secure favorable evaluations for those who perform them. The basic distributions of rank and influence thus tend to be the same at the end of the session as they were at the beginning and, in this sense, to remain stable. Differences in rank usually lead to parallel differences in the exercise of influence, and these latter in turn react back on and confirm the initial rank differences—this is the essence of a cycle of the process. Since each coming together of the members starts where the last left off, the over-all result is the appearance of a stable distribution of influence among the group's members.

There is a certain similarity between the principal effect of the process and a basic feature of complex authority structures. The process continually operates to maintain the commonly observed conjunction of rank and influence. A similar conjunction, between rank and power, occurs when the distribution of power in a complex organization is "legitimate" —that is, when power is held in accordance with the values of the organization and exercised in accordance with the norms defining its use—and the conjunction is thus a condition of the stable distribution of power among the organization's units. In an analogous way, the conjunction of rank and influence in the leadership structures of small groups forms a principal condition of a stable distribution of influence, for this conjunction also reflects the "legitimacy" of the distribution—that is, the degree to which influence is "possessed" in accordance with whatever values in the group justify its possession and exercised in accordance with whatever norms define the relevant behavior patterns.

The process joining rank and influence may therefore be viewed as contributing to the stability of the distribution of influence by continually recreating the condition of legitimacy. In this case, however, the norms and values forming an essential part of that condition are not fixed or "given." On the contrary, their degree of institutionalization, like that of other ideas in the group's consensus, is sustained or modified by the very behavior they legitimate, the exercise of influence, and they may be in consequence highly variable. For this reason the tendency toward legitimacy, which the process implies, may be realized in the conventional way—members' ranks are "given" or fixed and influence is distributed or redistributed among the members so as to parallel their ranks; but it may also be realized in the opposite way—the existing or evolving differences in influence become legitimated through a redistribution of ranks; or it may be realized by a simultaneous adjustment of both properties.

Despite the possible paths to legitimacy, the rank-influence process only tends to produce a stable distribution of influence; it does not necessarily do so. There are several reasons for this. Each property is directly or indirectly dependent on numerous factors outside the group's interaction system, and the process may be unable to counter the effects of external factors. It will tend to do so, but at any given time it may not in fact do so. Second, the process does not produce an "equilibrium" between rank and influence. It does not even tend to keep the size of the differences (among members) in rank and influence constant. At most it keeps the two properties coordinate. The development of ever larger or ever smaller differences in these respects among the members is thus entirely consistent with the operation of the process. And third, in the course of coordinating rank and influence, the process tends to produce side-effects, including decreasing the level of other fundamental group properties (for example, frequency of interaction) below the minimum point necessary for the group to continue.

With respect to the second reason, to discuss that first, there are two directional tendencies inherent in the process as depicted by the propositions. One, increasing inequalities among the members may develop—the rich may get richer and the poor, poorer—since nothing in the present formulation (with one minor exception noted below) implies a brake on the operation of the process. Rank differences may produce increasingly larger influence differences, which in turn produce increasingly larger rank differences, which in turn produce increasingly larger influence differences, and so on. Unless checked by other group processes or outside events, this cumulative increase in differences would eventually create too great a gap between the higher- and lower-ranking members for them to continue together as a small group.

Alternatively, adjustive tendencies may proceed in the opposite direction. The rich in this case may get so much poorer and the poor so much richer that neither inherits the group. This equalizing tendency also requires an external check, for without one, it would eventually erase effective differences among the members so far as rank is concerned, and thereby erase as well a principal (if not the principal) source of orderliness in interaction sequences in groups.

The possibility of such developments occurs, as was said, because nothing within the process restricts the amounts by which members may differ from one another in rank and influence. What converts the possibility into something highly probable is the fact that key elements in the process—centrality and conformity in particular, but rank as well—are dependent on factors external to the system. They are thus liable to vary in ways that from the perspective of the system appear to be random. Powerful nonmembers, for example, may simply elect to by-pass the group's higher-ranking members and deal directly with its middle-ranking members; this would be likely to produce in time a reranking of members and hence a redistribution of influence as well. Moreover, in the course of adjustments such as these, which entail first equalization and then differentiation, considerable confusion and temporary disorganization are likely to mark interaction sequences; and there is no necessary reason why a group would survive the transition. Or, to take another example, perhaps the leading members find their other membership commitments absorbing increasing amounts of their time and energy. Their centrality declines as a result, and in consequence so do their conformity, observability, influence, and rank. These adjustments might not in themselves occasion any confusion or disorganization, but they probably would if, after they had occurred, the outside commitments became less pressing and the former leading members were prepared to resume active participation in the group's affairs.

Environmental changes may of course induce or facilitate the differentiating tendency as well. For example, the lower-ranking members of a group may begin participating regularly in other groups in which there are norms counter to those in the first group. The effect of this would be to set in motion a steady decline in their relative conformity within the first group and hence to occasion parallel reductions in their relative influence, rank, centrality, and observability. The resulting degree of differentiation would be much larger than would otherwise have occurred.

Both developmental tendencies, the equalizing and the differentiating, occur *through* the operation of the rank-influence process, *not* in spite of it. This is so whether the triggering event is internal to the system or external. Yet the product of the process, the conjunction of rank and influence, is a condition of the stability of their distribution. The effective operation of the process thus constitutes a necessary condition of stability —for rank and influence would otherwise become dissociated— but not a sufficient condition, for even when the process operates effectively to bring about a legitimate distribution, it may create considerable instability. By implication, the same conclusion holds for the condition of legitimacy itself: without it, a distribution of influence will probably prove to be unstable, but even with it, and even in the short run, the distribution may still turn out to be unstable.

In a general way, perhaps, this formulation catches up the main elements one needs to take account of in an analysis of stability and instability in influence structures, but it has certain evident shortcomings. For one thing, it calls for a degree of interrelationship among the variables, a precision to the adjustive sequences, that ordinarily does not obtain. Certainly nothing in the data reported in Chapters 3 and 4, or for that matter, in our general empirical knowledge of groups, suggests that the usual relationships among the properties are strong enough to produce such nicely attuned repercussions as the model portrays. Also, it fails to deal with several matters of evident relevance and interest. For example, what are the effects on the process of differentiated leadership statuses? For when these are institutionalized, it is often the case that any one of several members may be the highest ranking and most central, depending on the circumstances and group activities.

In order to explore some of the implications of the model and to introduce into the analysis some additional considerations, the remainder of the chapter focuses on the differentiating tendency and asks, What processes or structural features of groups tend to facilitate this tendency and which tend to block it? [1]

Some Mechanisms Furthering the Differentiating Tendency

The occurrence of the differentiating tendency is rooted in the nature of the connection between influence and rank,

---

[1] The equalization tendency could as well provide the focus, of course, for, being opposite in direction, the tendencies are affected by the same factors but in contrary ways.

as described by Proposition 14. Actions that are influential are often also actions that are appraised as commendable, and hence they maintain or raise the member's rank. It is not necessary, of course, that a member be recognized as influential for him to have both high rank and much influence, nor is it necessary that the same actions that secure the one produce the other. But for an action that exemplifies group standards or expresses common sentiments to be influential to a more than ordinary degree, it must evidently be recognized by others for what it is. Such actions are especially influential precisely because they are seen to be good. The very quality that makes them influential thus contributes directly to the rank of the member performing them.

Among the mechanisms that promote increasing differentiation among group members with respect to rank and influence are the following.

The Relationship between Rank, Expected Performance, and Perceived Performance[2]

The recognition or perception of an action as "good" (or "bad") may result from an assessment of the action solely in terms of group standards. But far more often, it would seem, such an evaluation reflects less the merits of the action and more the rank of the member performing it. A series of studies carried out under the direction of Sherif provides systematic data on the operation of this important mechanism.

Harvey (1953) identified ten junior high school cliques for which both objective and subjective measures of rank were in perfect agreement. From each clique, the highest-, lowest-, and a middle-ranking member were asked to take part in the experiment. In each trio, while one member threw 50 darts,

---

[2] See "The Self-Fulfilling Prophecy" in Merton, 1957, pp. 421-436, for a detailed discussion of this mechanism and its application to the operation of ethnic stereotypes.

the other two recorded, first, their individual estimates of how well he would do and then, after the throw, their judgment of how well he had done. (Highly accurate judgments could be made.) The thrower did the same, calling his estimates and judgments aloud as well as recording them. Three D-scores, measuring the differences between estimates and judgments, were constructed for each position. The results show clearly the correlation between rank and *expected* performance.

Position Throwing	Positions Judging	Average of D-Scores
Leader	Leader	3.16 (overestimation)
	Middle	2.99
	Low	2.45
Middle	Leader	1.66
	Middle	2.49
	Low	.98
Low	Leader	−.13 (underestimation)
	Middle	−.18
	Low	.90

In this study, "subjects were able to estimate with very high accuracy the score actually made on each trial" (*ibid.*, pp. 361-362). In a subsequent experiment (Sherif *et al.*, 1955) a similar "task" was used, but this time the subjects threw hand-balls instead of darts and the face of the target was covered, thereby making it extremely difficult for the participants to judge accurately how well someone had thrown.

The subjects in this second study were two groups of 10 boys each. Each boy had 25 throws. After a member threw, his co-members recorded their individual judgments of how well he had thrown, the thrower called aloud what he guessed he had scored, and the experimenter recorded the actual score, which he could do very accurately. (Wired to each target area was a light, visible to him but not to the subjects, which flashed when the target area was hit.) D-scores giving the mean differences between actual and estimated scores were computed for each boy, and the boys in each group were ordered according to these D-scores. The boy whose actual performance was most overrated received rank 1, and the boy whose actual performance was most underrated received rank 10. These perceived performance "ranks" were correlated with the boys' group ranks. In both groups the rank-order correlation coefficient was about .7.[3]

Stated generally, the mechanism consists of two linked propensities. One is to expect a better performance from a higher-than a lower-ranking member, and the other is to perceive the outcome of performances as confirming the expectation. There are of course certain "realistic" restrictions on the operation of the mechanism. As Sherif's ingenious experiment demonstrates so clearly, it is when the actual outcome is ambiguous that the effect of expectation on perception is greatest. Furthermore, since the evaluations are collective in nature, it is social reality that most often provides the operative testing ground for an individual member's judgments. There is in consequence ample room for Asch effects to overcome any particular member's tendency to see the emperor as lacking clothes.

It is important to realize that this perceptual distortion is not limited to the case where performances by people with low ascribed rank are perceived as less satisfactory than performances by people with high ascribed rank. The mechanism describes a tendency inherent in all ranking systems, whatever the content of the standards used in making the evaluations. In a completely performance-oriented system, no less than in any other, it would still be the case that someone judged to have

---

[3] The exact r's are .737 and .676. I computed the rank-order correlation coefficients for actual performance and group rank, and for each group it was about zero (−.05 and .004), which makes the "task" especially suited to the purpose of the study.

done very well in the past (present rank) will be expected to do very well in his next performance and will probably be perceived as in fact doing well in it.[4]

The effect of the mechanism just described on the rank-influence process is obvious. Given objectively equal performances by high- and low-ranking members of a group, the action of the former is more likely than the action of the latter to be rated as especially good. High-ranking men thus need to do particularly poorly for some length of time in order to suffer a lowering of rank and need do only a little better than usual in order to raise it. A slightly off performance by a low-ranking man, however, lowers his relative rank, and only a markedly good one raises it. The result, stated in very general terms, is that rank differences are rather more easily maintained, or increased, than decreased. That a bias exists in most systems in favor of the occurrence of the differentiating tendency is an obvious derivation.

Mutual Support among Leaders

The relevance of the mechanism outlined above to the rank-influence process is heightened by the operation of another, the tendency for the leading members of a group to express in front of others only positive evaluations of one another.

---

[4] Barnard (1946) clearly recognized the phenomenon in performance-oriented ranking systems and, in fact, considered it the source of a major "pathology" in the rank systems of complex organizations. Parsons' radical reinterpretation of the Linton status vs. role distinction, and his translation of it into a pair of relative categories (qualities and performances) that can be exchanged for one another when shifts occur in the *time-scale* of the system under review (or, in the time perspective of the analyst), is also pertinent here. For if the psychological tendency under discussion in the text is to have *systematically* relevant sociological effects, it is obviously necessary that it be possible to "convert" performances into qualities: otherwise, present attainments could not become ascribed characteristics with respect to the next phase of interaction. And if that were not possible, the construct of a performance-centered ranking system would be a contradiction in terms.

Homans (1950) observes that "the sentiments of the leaders of a group carry greater weight than those of the followers in establishing a social ranking" (p. 181). This is an extremely important observation in the present context. Its rationale within the theory developed here is straightforward: Members' ranks, being a part of the group's normative consensus, are in principle affected by the exercise of influence no less than other elements of the consensus; and the higher-ranking members exercise more influence than others. Hence, in virtue of their rank at time 1, they are able to exert more influence than others on the rank they will be accorded at time 2.

By itself this is important for the maintenance of existing rank differences. But it is when two or more leading members regularly support one another "in public" that it plays an important part in generating rank differences. For owing to their high rank and high centrality, the leading members exercise among them practically all the influence exercised in the group. Consequently, should they form a working coalition, virtually all of the influence exerted on rankings is exerted in support of according them an increasingly higher relative rank.

By a working coalition here I do not mean a mutual admiration society, much less a conspiracy. It is probably enough in many cases for the leading members simply to avoid negatively sanctioning one another "in public" (that is, when other members are present). Whyte reports a characteristic instance:

> One night when the Nortons had a bowling match, Long John had no money to put up as his side bet, and he agreed that Chick Morelli should bowl in his place. *After the match* Danny said to Doc, "You should never have put Chick in there." Doc replied with some annoyance, "Listen, Danny, you yourself suggested that Chick should bowl instead of Long John." Danny said, "I know, but you shouldn't have let it go." (1943, pp. 258-259; emphasis added)

Although he personally had misgivings about it, Doc accepted Danny's suggestion rather than turn it down in front of the others, and Danny, although subsequently deciding his idea was a poor one, said nothing rather than correct Doc while others were present. It may have cost them a "bad decision," but the two leading members of the Nortons avoided negatively sanctioning one another in public.

These two mechanisms primarily affect differences in rank and contribute to the differentiating tendency in this way. Two others primarily affect differences in influence.

Rank and Support for New Ideas

Partly because of the two tendencies just discussed—for leading members to avoid sanctioning one another negatively in public and for the performances of leading members to be perceived as good—and partly for other reasons, leading members are much more likely than others to be positively sanctioned and much less likely to be negatively sanctioned. Since the incorporation of new ideas into the group's consensus depends on the support given to the ideas, and since leading members find it comparatively easy to mobilize positive support, they have a near monopoly on innovative influence.

From one point of view, this is just a special case of the connection leading from rank to influence, as stated in the theory so far. But from another, it is more than that, for in this case high rank leads to innovative influence fairly directly. The rank itself remains dependent on being relatively high on the other properties (centrality, observability, and conformity), but in the actual exercise of the influence these are facilitative at best—the greater the leading member's observability, for example, the less likely he is to propose a virtually unacceptable idea. They are not more than that, however, because the effect of the support which the leading member can mobilize in virtue of his rank is to create a shortcut from rank to influence. The intervening conditions are, as it were, by-passed, and influence derives almost directly from rank.

The Translation of Innovative Influence into Reinforcing Influence

Complementing this last mechanism is one by which innovative influence is "translated" into reinforcing influence and hence into higher rank. In the superb Part III of *Political Parties* ("The exercise of power and its psychological reaction upon the leaders"), Michels makes the point that leaders select courses of action for the organization on the sincere assumption that they are acting solely in the best interests of the organization, whereas it sometimes turns out that the courses chosen prove more beneficial to the leaders in relation to the organization than to the organization in relation to its public goals. The specific process Michels is discussing is to be found in complex political organizations of a particular stamp and is therefore far removed from our present concern. But in the effects of their actions, if not in their intentions, the leaders of small groups often act in a way that seems to parallel significantly the actions of Michels' political leaders. Whyte again provides an example:

> The leader need not be the best baseball player, bowler, or fighter, but he must have some skill in whatever pursuits are of particular interest to the group. It is natural for him to promote activities in which he excels and to discourage those in which he is not skilful; and, in so far as he is thus able to influence the group, his competent performance is a natural consequence of his position. At the same time his performance supports his position (1943, p. 259).

Because they exercise innovative influence, leading members increase their conformity relative to others, and because of this increase, they exercise more reinforcing influence—and in consequence, increase their rank relative to others as well.

Leader-Follower Role Differentiation

One more mechanism may be mentioned here, the devolution onto the leading members of distinctive, normatively defined "responsibilities." It was mentioned in Chapter 4 that the leadership role is probably the most common mechanism by which parallel distributions of all five properties are secured. This role also makes a special contribution to the braking of the equalizing tendency and to the development of the differentiating tendency.

As a brake on the equalizing tendency, and on the mild anarchy which that may produce, the mechanism is so familiar that it needs little discussion. Lippitt's report (1949) of a training course in human relations provides two simple instances of what happens when the minimal leadership rights and responsibilities are not clearly defined and assigned (ordinarily, they are). In both, rank differences sufficiently large to permit orderly interaction to go on were lacking. In the first, too little reinforcing influence (here, on procedural norms) was exercised, and in the second, no center of attention emerged.

The training course was run over several days, the participants meeting in three groups or workshops of from 14 to 17 members and a faculty leader. In the afternoon, the leader was usually absent for an hour or so, and one of the members was appointed to act in his place. On returning to his group one afternoon, the faculty leader asked for a discussion of the temporary leader's success:

> "Delegate 2: I think my first observation is that our leader did a swell job of getting us to define our goal for what we wanted to do during the period, but several times during the hour he let one of us lead the group astray without feeling he could take the initiative to call us back on the beam. I felt several times as though I wanted him to represent me in taking some initiative with other members of the group." (Lippitt, 1949, p. 129)

To which the temporary leader replied:

> "I felt that problem two or three times and didn't know what to do about it. I guess I was just insecure about stepping on somebody's toes and didn't think how others would be feeling if I didn't step on somebody's toes." (*ibid.* pp. 129)

In the evenings, discussions were held about the ways in which the workshops themselves operated, and in one of these sessions, a nonparticipant observer of the groups related the following incident:

> "At the end of the morning session, the leader didn't take his customary step of getting a member of the group chosen as leader for the afternoon session when he would be absent. This meant that when the group met after lunch there was no officially designated leader. . . . Two members of the group obviously were feeling some responsibility and need to see that things moved ahead . . . This led to some rather interesting confusions because some persons would address their remarks and ideas to one leader, and some would address their remarks to the other. Parts of the group seemed to be looking in one direction for leadership and parts in the other" (*ibid.* pp. 116-117).

The observer's report continues,

> "Finally, one of the members of the group seemed to sense the direction in which this was leading and did a very interesting thing. He not only suggested the need for officially designating the leader, but actually suggested functions for both of the two unofficial leaders by nominating one of them to coordinate the discussion and the other to act as recorder and get down the things said at the blackboard. Everybody in the group seemed to feel relieved at this suggestion, including the two leaders" (*ibid.* p. 117).

That it was a third member who proposed defining the responsibilities of the two contending members, and who therefore exercised influence, reflects the low degree of differentiation in this group (in the absence of the faculty leader). More commonly, the definition and redefinition of the leadership role results from the exercise of influence by the leading members themselves. It is this that makes simple leader-follower role differentiation an occasionally important stimulus to the differentiating tendency. For just as leading members tend to exercise influence in support of their ranks and in favor of ideas they already hold or of activities they do well, so they may also tend to exercise it in support of a definition of their role that helps to anchor or increase both their rank and their influence.

The effects are analogous to those Weber (1946) attributes to "legal guarantees" in the case of stratification by status group in the larger society, while the process itself bears a certain resemblance to the one Michels (1949) describes for complex organizations. Tendencies towards equalization are prevented by the bundling together of a variety of activities into a normatively defined role which only certain members, the higher-ranking, are permitted to play. If the role definition comprises the kinds of behaviors that are likely to prove influential in the group (such as the negative sanctioning of deviance) and those that promote centrality (such as indicating who may speak during a discussion and in what order), it can provide a kind of "guaranteed" pre-emption of the opportunities for exercising influence—"guaranteed" because it is a part of the group's consensus and hence maintained by the very capacity it creates.

The differentiating tendency, although rooted in the link between reinforcing influence and rank, and furthered by the kinds of mechanisms described here, is probably seldom carried to its logical conclusion, for reasons to be discussed shortly. But if it were, it would presumably end with the reconstitution of the group as a subset of the network of interpersonal relations that is organized around the person of the central member. For as rank and influence cumulate, so too does centrality, until the point is reached at which interaction goes almost solely between the highest-ranking member and each of the others. The structure of the group would thus come to resemble the "star" or "X" type of communications net, and the group as such would presumably disappear at about this point.[5]

Some Mechanisms Countering the Differentiating Tendency

Nothing within the general rank-influence process promotes equalization to the same extent as the direct relation between reinforcing influence and rank promotes the differentiating tendency. As will be seen below, though, some of the mechanisms countering differentiation may set in motion a downward spiral that, if not checked, would create a state of considerable disorganization in a group.

Effective Influence

It is an implication of the model that under certain conditions, the leading members may erase the differences between them

---

[5] A case reported in a paper by a student, Miss Beverly Rempel, is relevant here. Miss Rempel attended an acting school and was a member of a clique composed of peers who were greatly concerned with "the problems of the stage." One of their number was chosen to play the lead in the annual spring play and promptly became the most central person whenever the members got together. Apparently, all other lines of interaction simply stopped operating within the clique. In this case, her charisma wore off right after the third of the three performances, but the clique was permanently broken. A second case occurred in connection with a study group formed by several graduate students taking a particular course. It met once or twice a week to discuss the lectures and related problems. One participant was markedly more capable than the other four or five. The group soon ceased to meet at all because each of the others tended to seek out this one person in order to discuss alone with him ideas and problems related to the course and to the papers each was working on. These are only two cases, but they correspond in an impressionistic way to the eventual outcome of the "differentiating tendency."

and the others. For they may so successfully reinforce group opinion through their influential actions that the differences in conformity among the members of the group are progressively narrowed. Even if the differences do not in fact disappear, the narrowing reduces the rank differences also, and in due course the other differences as well. If the behaviors that usually constitute an exercise of influence (besides, of course, the simple exemplification of a group norm) are anchored by normative definitions in leadership roles, there can result a considerable discrepancy between rank differences and influence differences, thus creating pressures to modify the definitions of the leadership roles. Impressionistically, a development something like this appears to take place occasionally in training situations, where "pupils" become by the end of the program nearly as good as the "teachers."

Leadership Failures

Perhaps the most obvious brake on the differentiating tendency is ineffective leadership. As Whyte (1943) puts it, the leader's ideas must turn out to be "right," relative to the members' given motivations (p. 259). For of course, merely because a high-ranking member is influential is no guarantee that the ideas he supports by his influence are good ones.

Most groups, nuclear families perhaps being the major exception, engage considerably less of the person than is left outside the group, and what is not engaged provides the immediate context for what is. Even if a group is so important to its members severally that for each the maintenance of his membership is a relatively autonomous need or an ultimate personal value, the satisfaction of the need or the realization of the value is limited by his having to satisfy other needs and to realize other values. As was said earlier, these elements of participants' personalities that are outside the group proper form a composite "psychological environment," which sets certain immutable conditions of existence for the group as such, at least in the short run. The failure of the group to function effectively enough relative to these environmental conditions means simply that it fails to meet an important set of functional requirements. If the high-ranking and influential members' ideas are not "right," these requirements are not met.

In general, the existence of functional requirements implies only that the group will in time cease to exist if it is "inefficient," to use Barnard's term. It certainly implies no particular structural arrangements that effectively provide the differentiating tendency with a ceiling. Inadequate leadership brings to an end, then, not so much this development as the group itself. Consequently, while the failure of the leaders' ideas to be "right" certainly effects a halt in the cumulation of their rank and influence, it does so in a theoretically uninteresting way.

Leadership failures occur for a very large number of reasons, and there would be little point in trying to catalog them. The previous formulations imply two rather basic conditions that make failures inherent in certain structures, however, and it may be worth while to note them.

It was mentioned in the preceding section that there is a strong tendency to perceive performances in the light of the rank of the member who performs them. The more pronounced this tendency, the more inflated the rank differences: the members think of one another as differing in the relevant qualities and performance-capacities far more than they actually do. They thus tend to expect from the leading members increasingly better performances, with the result, eventually, that expectations develop which these members are not capable of meeting. Since, under most conditions, the leaders' actions cannot all be of the sort that has an ambiguous outcome, they at some point "fail."

The tendency for leading members to escape negative sanctioning the higher their rank also implies possible failure. For as they become progressively freed from the controls which their centrality ordinarily entails, they become necessarily less responsive to group opinion. The interaction they engage in is less informative and less constraining, and they consequently suffer a drop in both observability and conformity. In due course they become less influential and experience a decline in rank. But the adjustments may not occur before their de facto isolation causes them to blunder in a major way, in which case they would suffer a fairly precipitous decline in rank.

Leader-Follower Role Differentiation

The cumulation of rank and influence, and the increasingly unequal distribution of rewards that it implies, has serious effects on the lower-ranking members' motivations to take part in the group. If the development were to continue unchecked, these members would presumably become so apathetic that they would either withdraw on their own initiative or be asked to do so.

The principal device to reduce the strain of rank differences is, as Barnard (1946) points out, differentiation between leaders' and followers' roles and a corresponding differentiation of the standards by which their respective performances are evaluated:

> The necessity for differentiation from the standpoint of those of inferior ability is that without it they are constantly in a position of disadvantage, under pressure to exceed their capacities, perpetually losing in a race in which no handicaps are recognized, never able to attain expected goals so long as they are treated as the equals of those who in fact are superior; therefore they are always in a position of never securing respect for what they do contribute, of always incurring disrespect for what they cannot do (p. 61).

As was said in the preceding section, however, the differentiation of roles may itself contribute to further differentiation in rank and influence, in which case the group's level of solidarity may be reduced below the point necessary for its persistence as a group. This outcome is possible because, as rank and influence cumulate, so does centrality. Almost all interaction thus gets channeled into the relations between the highest-ranking member(s) and others, and almost all interaction is therefore organized through stably and highly differentiated roles. Members interact entirely, or almost entirely, as superiors and subordinates. The norms continually exemplified and reinforced through the operation of the group, therefore, are norms referring to *differences* between subclasses of members. Little or nothing occurs to exemplify and reinforce what is *common* to all members—except that they all hold in common the idea that they should be different. There may be consensus, but there is little cohesion or solidarity.

Subgroup Formation

A somewhat more interesting possibility is suggested by the following observation of Simmel (1950):

> The subordination of a group under a single person results, above all, in a very decisive unification of the group. This unification is almost equally evident in both of two characteristic forms of this subordination. First, the group forms an actual, inner unit together with its head; the ruler leads the group forces in their own direction, promoting and fusing them; superordination, therefore, here really means only that the will of the group has found a unitary expression or body. Secondly, *the group feels itself in opposition to its head and forms a party against him* (p. 190; emphasis added).

In order for lower-ranking members to form a "party" against the higher-ranking member(s), they must interact with one another. This raises certain difficulties that I will take up shortly. But if they do, the automatic effect is to reduce the high-ranking members' relative centrality. Since the lower-ranking members' interactions with one another occur most likely in the absence of the high-ranking members, the "party"

effectively reduces the latter's relative observability and conformity as well. The resulting reduction in rank differences may
occur in two ways. The high-ranking member(s) may remain
in the group and suffer the reductions to take place. Or they
may become, like deviants, defined as too different for continued inclusion as members. In the latter case the group's
membership boundaries are redrawn, the previously highest-
ranking members become members emeritus, and the subgroup of subordinates becomes the effective group.

The principal gap in the argument occurs at the point where
the "party" is to form against the high-ranking member(s).
The general process that enters here is that of subgroup formation and is too large a topic to be explored in this essay. It
seems likely, though, that in this case the dynamic is provided
by a side effect of the differentiation between leaders' and
followers' roles in conjunction with the followers' motivations
to participate.

Let us assume that low-ranking members' motivations can
be reduced but only so far; at a certain point they can be cut
down no further, perhaps because the members have certain
goals that can be achieved only through their participating in
the group. Let us also assume that the maintenance of motivation requires that occasionally sentiments of solidarity be expressed. If the differentiation has gone far, however, this requirement is not met. Since they must continue to participate,
the members feel a need to be motivated. What provides the
basis for the expression of sentiments of solidarity among the
lower-ranking members is precisely their common position of
subordination, their common characteristic of low rank.

This objectively common characteristic must be perceived
or felt, of course, in order to become operative, a matter that
raises a number of problems. But at the least such perception
is greatly facilitated by the distinctive role the higher-ranking
member plays toward them. He is seen to be different from
them and they see themselves as alike with respect to him.

This sheer awareness has a further consequence of relevance.

One tends to impute to one's assumed equals a greater degree of similarity to one's self than actually exists. Similarly, the sense of difference leads one to impute to those he assumes are different a greater degree of difference than actually exists.[6] The range of interaction with the higher-ranking member(s) is thus even more narrowly circumscribed than it need be. At the same time, the sense of similarity among the low-ranking members, by encouraging interaction among them, feeds into and becomes in time the sense of solidarity.

Thus, if the differentiating tendency reduces the lower-ranking members' motivations to participate too much, the formation of a cohesive subgroup of low-ranking members can counteract this effect and also control the differentiating development. But it does so at a cost, for subgrouping produces its effects through so altering the group's structure that it is no longer a "small" group, or through so redefining the group's membership boundaries that the higher-ranking personnel are no longer group members, or through so drastically starting a reranking downward tendency that an equalization development may set in.

Differentiated Leadership Roles

Another brake on the differentiating tendency, and probably the most effective, so far as over-all stability of group structure is concerned, is the parallel development of differentiated leadership roles. Once differentiated follower and leader roles

[6] A study by Sappenfield (1942) illustrates the way in which differences are characteristically overestimated. Members of three religious groups were asked to complete the Thurston-Peterson attitude-toward-communism scale and to say, if either Jews or Protestants, how Catholics would probably respond to each item, or if Catholics or Protestants, how Jews would probably respond. Jews turned out to be most favorable to communism and Catholics least favorable. But Catholic and Protestant students thought Jewish students were more favorable than they actually were, and Jewish and Protestant students thought Catholic students were less favorable than they actually were. Where similarity is assumed, there is a tendency to overestimate the actual similarities (e.g., Ausubel, 1955).

have evolved and their allocation among the members has been settled, the further differentiation and stable allocation of sub-types of leadership roles may effectively curtail the cumulation of rank and influence.

Two main types of leadership role differentiation seem common in small-scale systems. One effects a splitting off of instrumentally functional leadership activities from expressively functional leadership activities (see Bales and Slater, 1955, and Zelditch, 1955). The other does the same for leadership activities within the group versus representative activities.

As for the first, the complication of group life beyond the performance of a single, nonrecurrent, and short-run task, and the correlative development of three relatively distinct sets of functional requirements or problems, appear to be associated with corresponding structural differentiations.[7] In most small groups two fairly distinct substructures occur. In one, members play highly differentiated roles vis-à-vis one another and outside people, their role-behaviors in this case contributing to the group's "instrumental" functional requirements. In the other, members play relatively undifferentiated roles, their behaviors here contributing to the group's "expressive" functional requirements, especially the requirement of adequate solidarity. Ordinarily a group will alternate back and forth between these two substructures through phase movements.

Each substructure usually contains a differentiated leadership role. And it is also usually the case that *different members*

---

[7] The three classes of requirements are, in Barnard's terms "efficiency," "effectiveness," and "communication." They go under a variety of names, but have been found to exist by a variety of investigators. Summarily, they refer to the maintenance of stable relationships between the group and its psychological environment (maintenance of motivation), the maintenance of stable relationships with its social and physical environments (achievement of goals), and the maintenance of a stable social structure within the group (maintenance of consensus and solidarity). The motivational and solidarity requirements often appear to be met through the same set of actions, but this is only when the rewards sustaining motivation are not specifically differentiated. Competitively allocated rewards do not normally create cohesion.

play these different roles, although why this is so is not well understood. (See Slater, 1955; Bales and Slater, 1955; Zelditch, 1955; Bales, 1956; and Bales, 1958.) If these two leadership roles are present, however, and if different members play them, then clearly the differentiation of leadership roles functions to contain the differentiating tendency. For the rank and influence of the "leadership role" are now split between two members, each of whom is relatively central at different times over the group's operation.

Somewhat the same effect is produced by the differentiation of representative roles from leadership roles proper. Many have remarked the tendency for the higher-ranking members of a group to interact at a high rate with powerful or otherwise significant nonmembers. If it develops that a member's representative responsibilities increase as his rank increases, an automatic control on the tendency is built into the group's structure. For increasingly high centrality and increasingly frequent interaction with nonmembers at some point come into conflict. Either the high-ranking member pursues his associations with nonmembers, in which case he removes himself from the group enough for the adjustments to take place: relative centrality, influence, and, eventually, rank remain constant or decline. Or, he permits others to assume the highly valued representative roles and suffers in due course a decline in relative rank as a result.

Summary

In this chapter the concepts and propositions previously set forth have been interpreted as depicting a process, here called the rank-influence process, which is considered to be basic to the interaction system of a small group. The process continually distributes rank and influence among a group's members and has for its principal effect the maintenance of a high correlation between these two properties. It may well produce instability in the course of operating, however, either in its own right or as the agency through which external factors transmit disturbing effects, since it contains two inherent directional tendencies. It may operate to increase the differences among members in rank, centrality, conformity, observability, and influence; or it may operate to decrease the differences and to make members approximately equal in these respects.

After picturing in a general way the operation of the rank-influence process, the chapter has focussed on several mechanisms that tend to further or to hinder the working out of the differentiating tendency. Among the mechanisms considered were: the relationship between rank, expected performance, and perceived performance; mutual support among leading members; the relationship between rank and support for new ideas; the translation of innovative influence into reinforcing influence; leader-follower role differentiation; subgroup formation; and differentiated leadership roles.

[6]

A Summing Up and Epilogue

If the theory developed in these pages organizes successfully the facts reported at several points, or, and this remains to be seen, suggests correctly where to find others, it is owing, I think, to its basically functional point of view. As put to use here in the study of influence, this orientation contains the following assumptions and considerations.

Any type of social system can tolerate a certain degree of deviance. For each type a characteristic range exists within which the activities of the participants may depart from the norms of the system without occasioning any basic changes in the structure of the system. Departures outside of this range do, however, occasion fundamental structural changes, even, possibly, the dissolution of the particular system.

In small groups the main action that functions to prevent the departures from exceeding the system's range of toleration is the exercise of influence. It performs this function in two ways, although in both of them it does so by acting on the states of consensus. In one, the influential action so affects consensus that group opinion changes to keep up with the changes which situational factors are causing in activities. It thus reduces or prevents too much deviance by keeping norms in line with behavior. In the other, the influential action so affects consensus that group opinion becomes strong enough to prevent the too frequent performance of situationally probable but deviant activities. In the latter case it might be thought that influence modifies or blocks the potentially deviant activities directly, and from one point of view it may seem to do so. But in this essay it has all the while been assumed that, howevermuch influential actions may affect behavior, they do so through the effects they have on states of consensus.

That some members of a group appear to exercise much influence and others very little is owing to the operation of a process which continually distributes influential actions among the group's members. This process may or may not distribute similar degrees of influence among members from one time period to the next, but if it does, the group in question gives the appearance of having a stable structure of influence. To discover the constituents of the process shaping influence structures into varying forms and granting them varying degrees of stability has been the objective of this essay.

For reasons that derive in part from this view of influence and in part from the work of Barnard, Homans, and Merton, it seems likely that rank, centrality, observability, and conformity have a persisting impact on the distribution of influence among the members of small groups. Accordingly, interest has centered on the probable relations among these four and between each of them and influence. All five are conceived to be properties of the status of member and to characterize the several members of a particular group in varying degrees. The propositions assert that the five properties are positively related to one another, and so it should usually be the case that, for any member of a small group relative to other members, the more of any one of them he has, the more he has of the others.

Since the essay is short and its subject very complex, it has been necessary to sacrifice scope for coherence. Much that is relevant to the study of influence in the small group has been put to one side, such as popularity, or discussed briefly and only in pasing, such as role differentiation. And, probably, some things of relevance have simply been ignored through oversight. If titles were the place for qualification, this essay might be headed, "An inquiry concerning some matters pertaining to the exercise of influence in selected kinds of groups and situations."

The theory presented here is short not only on scope, however, but also on confirmation. It is not merely a partial theory, it is a merely plausible partial theory. Evidence on its principal assertions is presented from time to time, but it does not take an especially careful reading to disclose how shaky are its empirical supports at several points. Certain key propositions lack a factual basis altogether, while some others need theirs made a good deal firmer before they could be called tentatively confirmed. On balance, I would say that the theory stands to the events it is to explain about as the figure in a Gestalt experiment stands to the ground: Depending upon one's angle of vision, the theory appears either to organize much that is known about group influence processes or to form the empty space that sets off several outstanding bodies of fact. Most of the time, I should hasten to add, I see it in the first way.

The likelihood that verificational studies will become fashionable in sociology within the next decade seems slight. Research is expensive and most money will continue to go in the future where it has gone in the past, to applied social research. One can so shape applied studies that their findings bear on certain theoretical problems, but the decisive questions in the design and analysis of research, what information is to be collected and what collected information is to be analyzed, must be answered in ways that allow the researcher to examine in detail the particular actions, situations, or groups under study, rather than in ways that would allow him to test adequately a complex middle-range theory. Whatever verification can be built into primarily applied researches is all to the good, but for perfectly proper and obvious reasons, theoretic concerns *per se* must give way in such research to the detailed investigation of the particular subject the researcher has chosen to describe or analyze.

The many applied researches of the past and the probably even greater number to come are productive, however, of a very large number of facts. If there is to be a steady growth of the corpus of sociology, that is, a steady cumulation of *organized* sociological knowledge, the research results must be continually bundled together into medium-sized packages of acknowledged fact. The collection of the facts is the province of research, but the bundling together is the province of theory, whether it does this in its own right or as a preface to or summary of a research report. For theory must lay out in an orderly fashion the cells in which findings can be stored; otherwise there is no body of knowledge proper. Analytic theory to date certainly has provided the cells and some have been arranged in a logically justifiable manner. But it fails for the most part to provide the necessary directions concerning which facts, or, rather, classes of facts, are to go into which cells. In consequence, various studies seem to have much in common and to contain mutual implications, but it is almost never very clear what exactly they do have in common or what exactly they do mutually imply. Things are roughly alike, approximately the same, seemingly different. They are all too seldom intentional modifications, evident replications, or flat contradictions. In such a vague world well-founded general statements of fact are very hard to find.

An organized body of knowledge, however, implies just the opposite. Precisely because the knowledge is organized one can move systematically about among the known facts, from the particular to the general and back again and from one set of facts to another. If it is to provide this sort of organization, analytic theory in sociology needs to go beyond the devising of generalized categories and the joining of them into occasional abstract propositions. It needs to take on the additional task of spelling out in considerable detail the kinds of events a category pertains to and, in particular, the kinds of evidence which would support the propositions. In short, although verificational research proper appears to be a long way off, the theorist needs to ready his ideas for testing, since in so doing he provides what is now missing, instructions about where to file research results.

There are, I think, five main steps to take in readying a theory for use. One, the events it explains occur within a setting, and this setting is described. (Here is where a standardized classification of social systems would save a great deal of time and trouble.) Two, the concepts of the theory proper are discussed in terms pertinent to their measurement. Three, the principal propositions are set down simply and clearly. Four, if available, evidence relevant to each of them is summarized in detail, not merely referred to in passing, so as both to suggest the plausibility of the assertion in question and to guide subsequent applications of it. Five, the set of assertions is applied to some case or class of cases in order to illustrate how the theory may be used in interpretation.

So to present a theory, of course, is to prepare it for disconfirmation as well as for confirmation. No one particularly likes to be wrong, especially one who has spent much effort in devising and communicating a complex of ideas that to him appears eminently reasonable. But a theory contains within it the seeds of its own disproof in any case. Insofar as it says anything about reality, it may to that extent say wrong things. If the theory is valid and viable, it will not only withstand presentation in this form but be strengthened by it. If it should contain misleading assumptions or erroneous assertions, the demonstration of its inadequacies is made easier, and it can be amended or discarded accordingly.

List of Works Cited

The following abbreviations are used in this list:

ASR: *American Sociological Review*

Group Dynamics: Dorwin Cartwright and Alvin Zander, eds., *Group Dynamics: Research and Theory.* Evanston, Ill.: Row, Peterson, 1953.

JASP: *Journal of Abnormal and Social Psychology*

JSP: *Journal of Social Psychology*

Readings in Social Psychology: Guy E. Swanson, Theodore M. Newcomb, and Eugene L. Hartley, eds., *Readings in Social Psychology.* New York: Holt, 1952.

Small Groups: A. Paul Hare, Edgar F. Borgatta, and Robert F. Bales, eds., *Small Groups: Studies in Social Interaction.* New York: Knopf, 1955.

Arensberg, Conrad M., and Solon T. Kimball, *Family and Community in Ireland.* Cambridge, Mass.: Harvard University Press, 1940.

Asch, S. E., "Effects of group pressure upon the modification and distortion of judgments," in Harold Guetzkow, ed., *Groups, Leadership, and Men*, Pittsburgh: Carnegie Press, 1951.

Asch, S. E., *Social Psychology.* New York: Prentice-Hall, 1952, Chapter 16.

Ausubel, D. P. "Socioempathy as a function of sociometric status in an adolescent group," *JASP*, 8(1955): 75-84.

Bales, Robert F., *Interaction Process Analysis.* Cambridge, Mass.: Addison-Wesley Press, 1950.

Bales, Robert F., "Some uniformities of behavior in small social systems," *Readings in Social Psychology*, 1952, 146-159.

Bales, Robert F., "The equilibrium problem in small groups," Chapter 4 of Talcott Parsons, Robert F. Bales, and Edward A. Shils, *Working Papers in the Theory of Action.* Glencoe, Ill.: The Free Press, 1953.

Bales, Robert F. "A theoretical framework for interaction process analysis." *Group Dynamics*, 1953, 30-38.

Bales, Robert F., "Task status and likeability as a function of talking and listening in decision-making groups," in Leonard D. White, ed., *The State of the Social Sciences*, Chicago: University of Chicago Press, 1956, 148-161.

Bales, Robert F., "Task roles and social roles in problem-solving groups," in Eleanor E. Maccoby, et al., eds., *Readings in Social Psychology*, 3rd Edition, New York: Henry Holt & Company, 1958, 437-447.

Bales, Robert F., and Philip E. Slater, "Role differentiation in small decision-making groups," Chapter 5 of Talcott Parsons, *et al.*, *Family, Socialization, and Interaction Process*. Glencoe, Ill.: The Free Press, 1955.

Bales, Robert F., Fred L. Strodtbeck, Theodore M. Mills, and Mary Roseborough, "Channels of communication in small groups," *ASR*, 16(1951): 461-468.

Banks, J. A., "The group discussion as an interview technique," *Sociological Review*, 5(1957): 75-84.

Barnard, Chester I., *The Functions of the Executive*. Cambridge, Mass.: Harvard University Press, 1938.

Barnard, Chester I., "The functions and pathology of status systems in formal organizations," in William F. Whyte, ed., *Industry and Society*. New York: McGraw-Hill, 1946, 46-83.

Bass, B. M., "An analysis of the leaderless group discussion," *JASP*, 33(1949): 527-533.

Bates, A. P. and J. S. Cloyd, "Toward the development of operations for defining group norms and member roles," *Sociometry*, 19(1956): 26-39.

Bavelas, Alex, "Communication patterns in task-oriented groups," in Daniel Lerner and Harold D. Lasswell, eds., *The Policy Sciences*. Stanford, Calif.: Stanford University Press, 1951, 193-202.

Berkowitz, Leonard, "Sharing leadership in small, decision-making groups." *Small Groups*, 1955, 543-555.

Berkowitz, Leonard, "Personality and group position," *Sociometry*, 19(1956): 210-222.

Borgatta, Edgar F., "Analysis of social interaction and sociometric perception," *Sociometry*, 17 (1954): 7-32.

Chapple, E. D., with the collaboration of C. M. Arensberg, *Measuring Human Relations* (Genetic Psychology Monographs, Vol. 22 (1940)).

Chowdhry, Kamla, and Theodore M. Newcomb, "The relative abilities of leaders and non-leaders to estimate opinions of their own groups." *Small Groups*, 1955, 235-245.

Cohen, Albert K., *Delinquent Boys: The Culture of the Gang.* Glencoe, Ill.: The Free Press, 1955.

Durkheim, Emile, *The Division of Labor in Society.* Glencoe, Ill.: The Free Press, 1947.

Durkheim, Emile, *The Rules of Sociological Method.* Glencoe, Ill.: The Free Press, 1950.

Durkheim, Emile, *Suicide: A Study in Sociology.* Glencoe, Ill.: The Free Press, 1951.

Feld, M. S., "Information and authority: the structure of military organization," *ASR*, 24(1959): 15-22.

Festinger, Leon, "Informal social communication." *Group Dynamics*, 1953, 190-203.

Festinger, Leon, and H. A. Hutte, "An experimental investigation of the effect of unstable interpersonal relations in a group," *JASP*, 49(1954): 513-522.

Festinger, Leon, Stanley Schachter, and Kurt Back, "The operation of group standards." *Group Dynamics*, 1953, 204-222.

Fortes, M. and E. E. Evans-Pritchard, eds., *African Political Systems*, London: Oxford University Press for the International African Institute, 1940.

French, Robert L., "Sociometric status and individual adjustment among naval recruits," *Group Dynamics*, 1953, 519-531.

Gage, N. L. and R. V. Exline, "Social perception and effectiveness in discussion groups," *Human Relations*, 6(1953): 381-396.

Goldberg, S. C., "Three situational determinants of conformity to social norms," *JASP*, 49(1954): 325-329.

Goldberg, S. C., "Influence and leadership as a function of group structure," *JASP*, 51(1955): 119-122.

Goode, William J., "A theory of role strain," *ASR* 25(1960): 483-496.

Gorden, R. L., "Interaction between attitude and the definition of the situation in the expression of opinion." *Group Dynamics*, 1953, 163-176.

Gross, Neal, Ward S. Mason, and Alexander W. McEachern, *Explorations in Role Analysis.* New York: Wiley, 1957.

Hare, A. Paul, "Interaction and consensus in different sized groups." *Group Dynamics*, 1953, 507-518.

Hare, A. Paul, "Small group discussions with participatory and supervisory leadership." *Small Groups*, 1955, 556-560.

Harvey, O. J., "An experimental approach to the study of status relations in informal groups," *ASR*, 18(1953): 357-367.

Heise, George A., and George A. Miller, "Problem solving by small groups using various communication nets." *Small Groups*, 1955, 353-367.

Hites, R. W., and D. T. Campbell, "A test of the ability of fraternity leaders to estimate group opinion." *JSP*, 32(1950): 95-100.

Homans, George C., *The Human Group*. New York: Harcourt Brace, 1950.

Homans, George Caspar, *Social Behavior: Its Elementary Forms*, New York: Harcourt, Brace & World, Inc., 1961.

Horsfall, A. B., and C. M. Arensberg, "Teamwork and productivity in a shoe factory." *Human Organization*, 8(1949): 13-28.

Hurwitz, Jacob I., Alvin F. Zander and Bernard Hymovitch, "Some effects of power on the relations among group members." *Group Dynamics*, 1953, 483-492.

Hyman, Herbert H., *Political Socialization: A Study in the Psychology of Political Behavior*. Glencoe, Ill.: The Free Press, 1959.

Kahn, Robert L., and Daniel Katz, "Leadership practices in relation to productivity and morale." *Group Dynamics*, 1953, 612-628.

Katz, Elihu, and Paul F. Lazarsfeld, *Personal Influence*. Glencoe, Ill.: The Free Press, 1955.

Lazarsfeld, Paul F. and Robert K. Merton, "Friendship as a social process: a substantive and methodological analysis," in Morroe Berger, et al., eds., *Freedom and Control in Modern Society*. New York: Van Nostrand, 1954, 18-66.

Leavitt, Harold J., "Some effects of certain communications patterns on group performance," *JASP*, 46(1951): 38-50.

Lennard, Henry L. and Arnold Bernstein, *The Anatomy of Psychotherapy: Systems of Communication and Expectation*, New York: Columbia University Press, 1960.

Lewin, Kurt, *Field Theory in Social Science*. New York: Harper, 1950.

Lewin, Kurt, "Group decision and social change." *Readings in Social Psychology*, 1952, 459-473.

Lewin, Kurt, Ronald Lippitt, and Ralph K. White, "Patterns of aggressive behavior in experimentally created social climates," *JSP*, 10 (1939): 271-299.

Linton, Ralph, *The Study of Man: An Introduction*, New York: Appleton-Century-Crofts, Inc., 1936.

Lippitt, Ronald, *Training in Community Relations*. New York: Harper, 1949.

Lippitt, Ronald, Norman Polansky, Fritz Redl, and Sidney Rosen, "The dynamics of powers." *Group Dynamics*, 1953, 462-482.

Lippitt, Ronald, and Ralph K. White, "An experimental study of leadership and group life." *Readings in Social Psychology*, 1952, 340-355.

Maier, N. R. F., and A. R. Solem, "The contribution of a discussion leader to the quality of group thinking: the effective use of minority opinions." *Group Dynamics*, 1953, 561-572.

March, James G., "An introduction to the theory and measurement of influence," *The American Political Science Review*, 49(1955): 431-451.

March, James G., "Influence measurement in experimental and semi-experimental groups," *Sociometry*, 19(1956): 260-271.

Merei, Ferenc, "Group leadership and institutionalization." *Readings in Social Psychology*, 1952, 318-328.

Merton, Robert K., "The role-set: problems in sociological theory," *The British Journal of Sociology*, 8(1957): 106-120.

Merton, Robert K., *Social Theory and Social Structure*. Glencoe, Ill.: The Free Press, 1957.

Michels, Robert, "The Origins of Anti-Capitalistic Mass Spirit" (1926), in *Man in Contemporary Society*. New York: Columbia University Press, 1955, 740-765.

Michels, Robert, *Political Parties*. Glencoe, Ill.: The Free Press, 1949.

Nadel, S. F., *The Theory of Social Structure*. London: Cohen & West, 1957.

Nagel, Ernest, "Teleological explanation and teleological systems," in Herbert Feigl and May Brodbeck, eds., *Readings in the Philosophy of Science*. New York: Appleton-Century-Crofts, 1953, 537-558.

Nagel, Ernest, *Logic Without Metaphysics*. Glencoe, Ill.: The Free Press, 1957.

Norfleet, Bobbie, "Interpersonal relations and group productivity," *Journal of Social Issues*, 4(1948), no. 2, 66-69.

Parsons, Talcott, *The Social System*. Glencoe, Ill.: The Free Press, 1951.

Parsons, Talcott, and Edward A. Shils, "Values, motives, and systems of action," in Parsons and Shils, eds., *Toward a Gen-*

eral Theory of Action. Cambridge, Mass.: Harvard University Press, 1952, 45-275.

Preston, Malcolm G., and Roy K. Heintz, "Effects of participatory vs. supervisory leadership on group judgment." *Group Dynamics*, 1953, 573-584.

Redl, Fritz, "Group emotion and leadership," *Psychiatry*, 5(1942): 573-596.

Riecken, Henry W., and George C. Homans, "Psychological aspects of social structure." Chapter 22 of Gardner Lindzey, ed., *Handbook of Social Psychology, Vol. II: Special Fields and Applications.* Cambridge, Mass.: Addison-Wesley, 1954.

Roethlisberger, F. J., and William J. Dickson, with the assistance and collaboration of Harold A. Wright, *Management and the Worker: An Account of a Research Program Conducted by the Western Electric Company, Hawthorne Works, Chicago.* Cambridge, Mass.: Harvard University Press, 1939.

Sappenfield, B. R., "The attitudes and attitude estimates of Catholic, Protestant, and Jewish students," *JSP*, 16(1942): 173-197.

Schachter, Stanley, "Deviation, rejection and communication." *Group Dynamics*, 1953, 223-248.

Seashore, Stanley, *Group Cohesiveness in the Industrial Work Group.* Ann Arbor, Mich.: Survey Research Center, Institute for Social Research, University of Michigan, 1954.

Shaw, M. E., "Some effects of unequal distribution of information upon group performance in various communication nets," *JASP*, 49(1954): 547-553.

Shaw, M. E., et al., "Decision processes in communication nets," *JASP*, 54(1957): 323-330.

Sherif, Muzafer, *The Psychology of Social Norms.* New York: Harper, 1936.

Sherif, Muzafer, "A preliminary experimental study of inter-group relations," John H. Rohrer and Muzafer Sherif, eds., *Social Psychology at the Crossroads.* New York: Harper, 1951.

Sherif, Muzafer and Carolyn W. Sherif, *An Outline of Social Psychology*, Rev. Ed., New York: Harper & Bros., 1956.

Sherif, Muzafer, B. Jack White, and O. J. Harvey, "Status in experimentally produced groups," *American Journal of Sociology*, 60 (1955): 370-379.

Simmel, Georg, *The Sociology of Georg Simmel.* Glencoe, Ill.: The Free Press, 1950.

Slater, Philip E., "Role differentiation in small groups." *Small Groups*, 1955, 498-515.

Steinzor, Bernard, "The spatial factor in face to face discussion groups." *Small Groups*, 1955, 348-353.

Stephan, Frederick F., and Elliot G. Mishler, "The distribution of participation in small groups: an exponential approximation," *ASR*, 17(1952): 598-608.

Strodtbeck, Fred L., "The family as a three-person group," *ASR*, 19 (1954): 23-29.

Talland, G. A., "The assessment of group opinion by leaders and their influence on its formation," *JASP*, 49(1954): 431-434.

Torrance, E. Paul, "Some consequences of power differences on decision-making in permanent and temporary three-man groups." *Small Groups*, 1955, 482-492.

Travers, R. M. W., "A study in judging the opinions of groups," *Archives of Psychology*, #266(1941).

Wallen, R., "Individuals' estimates of group opinion," *JSP*, 17(1943): 269-274.

Wallis, W. Allen and Harry V. Roberts, *Statistics: A New Approach*, Glencoe, Ill.: The Free Press, 1956.

Weber, Max, "Class, status, and party," in *From Max Weber: Essays in Sociology*. New York: Oxford University Press, 1946, 180-195.

Weber, Max, *The Theory of Social and Economic Organization*. New York: Oxford, 1947.

Whyte, William F., *Street Corner Society: The Social Structure of an Italian Slum*. Chicago, Ill.: The University of Chicago Press, 1943.

Zander, Alvin and A. R. Cohen, "Attributed social power and group acceptance: a classroom experimental demonstration," *JASP*, 51(1955): 490-492.

Zelditch, Morris, Jr., "Role differentiation in the nuclear family: a comparative study," Chapter 6 of Talcott Parsons *et al.*, *Family, Socialization, and Interaction Process*. Glencoe, Ill.: The Free Press, 1955.

Zetterberg, Hans L., "Compliant actions," *Acta Sociologica* 2(1957): 179-201.

Zetterberg, Hans L., *On Theory and Verification in Sociology*, Rev. ed. Totowa, N.J.: The Bedminster Press, 1963.

Name Index

Subject Index